The Trans Partner Handbook

of related interest

Trans Voices
Becoming Who You Are
Declan Henry
Foreword by Stephen Whittle, OBE
Afterword by Jane Fae
ISBN 978 1 78592 240 4
eISBN 978 1 78450 520 2

Transitioning Together
One Couple's Journey of Gender and Identity Discovery
Wenn B. Lawson and Beatrice M. Lawson
ISBN 978 1 78592 103 2
eISBN 978 1 78450 365 9

Straight Expectations
The Story of a Family in Transition
Peggy Cryden, LMFT
ISBN 978 1 78592 748 5
eISBN 978 1 78450 537 0

The Voice Book for Trans and Non-Binary People
A Practical Guide to Creating and Sustaining Authentic Voice and Communication
Matthew Mills and Gillie Stoneham
ISBN 978 1 78592 128 5
eISBN 978 1 78450 394 9

Can I Tell You About Gender Diversity?
A guide for friends, family and professionals
CJ Atkinson
Illustrated by Olly Pike
ISBN 978 1 78592 105 6
eISBN 978 1 78450 367 3

The Trans Partner Handbook

A Guide for When Your Partner Transitions

Jo Green

Jessica Kingsley *Publishers*
London and Philadelphia

Contains public sector information licensed under the Open Government Licence v3.0.

First published in 2017
by Jessica Kingsley Publishers
73 Collier Street
London N1 9BE, UK
and
400 Market Street, Suite 400
Philadelphia, PA 19106, USA

www.jkp.com

Library of Congress Cataloging in Publication Data
A CIP catalog record for this book is available from the Library of Congress

British Library Cataloguing in Publication Data
A CIP catalogue record for this book is available from the British Library

ISBN 978 1 78592 227 5
eISBN 978 1 78450 503 5

Printed and bound in Great Britain

To Angela, I love you.

Acknowledgements

To all the people who contributed your stories to the book, thank you for being so open and honest about your experiences; without you, this book would not have been possible.

To the Distinction members, thank you for reminding me how much this book is needed.

To Angela, thank you for letting me use our experiences to form the starting point for the book. Thank you for letting me share our story. Thank you for being a sounding board and my resident trans expert. Thanks for constantly reminding me that I am an author and that I can do this. Without you, none of this would have been possible.

Contents

Preface

I am the partner of a trans woman. My wife transitioned a number of years ago (but when exactly – that depends on when you start counting). All throughout her transition, I was adamant that I would support her. I have tried to find resources to help me get my head around everything that was happening, but anything that was available was largely aimed at being a good ally.

But, for me, being the partner of a trans person means that you are more than just an ally. You are an integral part of the transition process. You aren't just along for pride marches; you're there in the weeds. You're up at 2 a.m. holding your partner when their dysphoria is unbearable; you're there helping them research all the possible ways to make them feel better; you're there when they're hoping desperately for the right answer from the clinicians; you're there in the long stretches between appointments; you're there waiting for them when they're in surgery (hoping beyond hope that they'll be okay and that this will make it all right). You're the person they depend on. You're also there the first time they try out a new hairstyle, when they notice the changes in their body and can't stop smiling, when they start hormones for the first time, and when they get correctly gendered by a stranger. You're there to watch them grow into the more complete, more honest parts of themselves. You're there through all of it. You are more than just an ally.

I think it's important to highlight the experiences of people whose partners are trans. I also want to provide a guide for what to expect during transition and how to manage some of the complicated and confusing feelings that partners often go through. That's what this book is about. It's a book that I would have given myself 20 years ago.

This book is primarily for people who are in a relationship with a trans person. The focus on partners is because that's what my own history is, although you may also find it useful if you're a parent of a trans person or a supportive ally.

I have tried as far as possible to include all aspects of transition, for trans women, trans men and non-binary people too. I am mindful that every person's journey is different. This book is not the be-all and end-all for how transitions work and what happens. It's intended to be a starting point. It's a place where you can get some of the basics, so you have the background to open up the conversation.

Not all the experiences I cover here are universal, and many of them may not apply to you or your partner. Not all the steps that I list as part of transition will apply to your partner because every person's journey is different. In this book I've tried to give a practical approach to what sorts of things a person in a relationship with a trans person can expect. I'm not here as a single voice for trans people or a single voice for all partners of trans people. I'm just here, with my experience – backed up by research or professionals if needed – trying to make the world a slightly easier and less confusing place for you.

This book is also not the final word on everything trans and trans relationships; none of this is intended to replace discussion and exploration. The key to ensuring that your relationship with a trans person (and with anyone else, for that matter) works is communication. Keep talking, and enjoy the journey.

Part 1

The **PARTNER EXPERIENCE**

1

Introduction

Being a person whose partner is trans can be complicated. There is a whole host of new information that you'll need to come to grips with relating to language, pronouns and identity politics. You'll find yourself in the position of being a quasi-medical expert as well as an administration guru – all this while navigating your own identity and questions about sexuality and self-definition that you may never have considered before.

You may feel uncertain about the future, not really understanding what will happen and what the effects of the possible hormones and surgeries are going to be, alongside trying to figure out what this means for you, your family, your friends and the universe of people that you inhabit.

It is okay to feel a bit overwhelmed; the key thing to remember is that you will get through this. Allow your love to carry you through the harder times, and don't forget to celebrate the small things. It'll all turn out okay in the end.

Contributions

The book includes contributions from current partners of trans people and one former partner. Their identities vary across the spectrum and are representative of people whose partners also identify throughout the gender spectrum and are in various stages of their transitions.

Where people have requested anonymity, names have been replaced with pseudonyms that are kept consistent throughout the book. The contributions are included as they have been provided, with only minor edits to provide context/clarity. As a matter of course, I have anonymised the names of trans people, companies and clinicians.

The contributions are straightforwardly identified and are placed to show a partner's experience in that specific context.

"I believe that I fell in love with the person and the personality – my wife's personality hasn't changed; she is simply happier in herself (not always with how she looks but definitely in the fact that she gets to live how she wants/feels)." (Stevie)

Disclaimers (mainly though not exclusively about language use)

This book covers trans women, trans men and non-binary people. Recognising that all trans people are different, I have used the gender-neutral pronouns "they/them/their" in all the sections where I refer to trans people in the third person. This is specifically so that non-binary people are not erased in the discussions of hormones/surgery/etc.

Because this book is aimed at partners, this does mean that trans people are referred to in the third person in some sections. I do not intend to contribute to othering trans people, but in this specific context, I feel it's important to centre the partners' experiences.

In terms of referring to previous genders, I acknowledge that no matter how I write, the language is clunky and very binary. I am going to have to refer to people's assigned genders at birth at times, but where I do that, I've tried to be as sensitive as possible rather than opting for the medical language of hormones and genitalia.

I'm also in a monogamous relationship, which means that I write from that specific point of view. I recognise that there are polyamorous relationships with trans people, and for some people, a poly relationship is right for them. To try to make the book as practical as possible, I have had to write from the perspective of a partner to one person who is transitioning, but that doesn't mean that other partners are excluded. Other non-monogamous relationships are entirely valid; I just don't have the experience to write about them.

I refer to transition and the transition process and present the information in a linear, time-based way. This is to simplify what can be a confusing process for people. It doesn't mean that I'm dictating the right way or the only way. Every person is different, and their needs, approaches and decisions are also different.

None of the advice that I give should be taken instead of that of a medical professional or a counsellor. I am not a medical professional or a qualified counsellor, and I would advise that you seek out both medical and counselling help in relation to your partner's transition.

What does trans mean?

The language used in trans communities is ever changing and has evolved significantly in the last 50 years.

Initially, *transsexual* was the term most commonly used by the medical profession. It rose to prominence when Harry Benjamin, MD, published the book *The Transsexual Phenomenon* in 1966 (Benjamin, 1966). In it, Benjamin identified transsexualism as a medical disorder and outlined how the medical establishment should treat trans people. Much of the current medical transition process is based on Benjamin's principles.

During this time, an alternative term was being proposed by John F. Oliven (Oliven, 1965) – namely, *transgender*. Oliven makes the distinction that gender dysphoria is not concerned with sex but rather with gender.

The two terms continued to be used, with many debates centring on the use of the two words. Some people reject the term *transsexual* and prefer to identify as *transgender* because they transition their gender, not their sexuality, which is in keeping with Oliven's description. For others, *transsexual* indicates specifically people who require surgery (and are thus transitioning their identities), whereas *transgender* is an umbrella term that encapsulates all people who in any way don't conform to societal norms of gender (and thus includes people who cross-dress as well as people who transition into a different gender from what they were assigned at birth).

As a way to differentiate transgender people from people who aren't, the word *cisgender* is used (along with the shortened form *cis*). *Cis-* is a Latin-derived prefix which means "on the side of" and is effectively the opposite of *trans*. *Cisgender* refers to people whose gender identity matches the gender that they were assigned at birth.

The current usage of the word *transgender* most often refers to the community as a whole, and thus it is an umbrella term that includes anyone who self-identifies within the community. In keeping with this identification, *transgender* is an adjective, so it should be used to describe a person or a group of people. Lastly, the term *transgendered* is not preferred.

To get around the debate, a new term which started to see more common use was *trans**. The asterisk was used to represent a wild card and was seen to be inclusive of people who identify as transsexual, transgender, transvestite or intersex as well as people who don't feel that they fit the standard binary view of gender and even allies. This has changed over time, and the use of the asterisk has fallen out of favour in some trans communities.

The current trend is to just use the word *trans* (the shortened form of transgender). *Trans* is used to reflect this inclusive view of all gender-variant people but is more commonly associated with people who redefine their gender as something different to the gender that was assigned at birth and live in that redefined gender. Thus this term includes, for example, non-binary people, but excludes people who change their gender temporarily for specific performances (such as drag kings and drag queens).

I use *trans* throughout this book to refer to people who are transitioning their gender identities; a trans woman is a woman who is now living as a woman but was assigned male at birth, a trans man is a man who was assigned female at birth, and so on. Generally, I refer to people who have changed their gender identities as trans people.

The language can be complicated and is sometimes very confusing, because each person will define the way they use the language based on their own experience and their communities.

Gender and sex

In its simplest explanation, there is a difference between gender and sex. Generally, it's accepted that sex is the body and gender is what's inside. Most people can get their heads around this idea of being "born in the wrong body" and needing to change the body to better fit the feelings inside. This feeling of wrongness, of a trans person's body not matching how they see themselves, is called gender dysphoria.

> "I've learnt so much over the last couple of years. I've come to understand that sex and gender are different things; sex is biological and assigned at birth based solely on what is between the baby's legs, [while] gender is about what's between their ears and who they are or will be. Both are completely separate from sexuality, which is the mysterious business of attraction and who you will fall in love with. Neither gender nor sexuality are binary; both can be seen as a spectrum, which makes sense when you consider that you get very girly girls and other girls that live in jeans and have no desire to conform to any gender stereotypes and also get men varying from one end of the scale of macho to the other! That is not what it is to be transgender; this is not simply a case of a not particularly

butch guy wanting to wear dresses and deciding to become a girl in order to do so!" (Helen)

Gender exists beyond the mind. It infiltrates all areas of life and can be hugely different depending on cultural norms and individual circumstances.

Gender assigned at birth

A concept that's important to come to grips with is that gender is assigned at birth. When a baby is born, the doctor or midwife (or other person attending the birth) will assign a gender based on the presence of what appears to be a vagina or a penis. This assumes that people's genders are connected to their physical anatomy.

Some people are born intersex; that is, with genitals that are ambiguous or not clearly defined. These children are sometimes surgically changed very soon after the birth to make their genitals conform to what a doctor expects a vagina or a penis to look like. This is done with parental consent but without the child's consent. While intersex conditions are not specifically covered in this book, it's important to note that ambiguous genitalia in infants is estimated at 1 in 2000 babies born alive in the US (Ford, 2000). In these cases, when the child's genitalia are changed, it is most commonly altered to a vagina, as this is easier to produce surgically (Ford, 2000).

The other thing to note is that there are also chromosomal differences between people. There is a common myth that people have either XX (and thus female) or XY (and thus male) chromosomes. While this may be true for most people, there are variations. The World Health Organization (WHO) defines a number of variations to this; some people are sex monosomic (they have either an X or a Y chromosome but not both) and some people are sex polysomic (they have configurations such as XXX, XYY and XXY). The WHO also notes that there are some females who are born with XY chromosomes and some males who are XX (World Health Organization, 2016). The chromosomal variations are seemingly endless.

Why are people trans?

One of the key questions that people often want answered is why someone is trans. There is some research into what makes people trans, which is what this section will cover. It's important to know, however, that although there is research into what causes someone to be trans, that research is not perfect and is based on the fundamental idea that being trans is not "normal".

> "I've never questioned a person's reason for their choice to come out as transgender or to actually go through the transition process. It's not for me to say what is right for another. I have always just accepted that we're each hardwired differently, though more recently I have seen more research that suggests that we really *are* different and that a trans person's brain is more like the sex they identify with. I'm excited to see where this research goes. I believe that gender identity and sexual preference are genetic. I have seen families with multiple LGBTQ members, including my own. My own partner has multiple LGBTQ family members as well, including a relative who is in the process of transitioning." (Julia)

As a partner, it may be comforting to know that a person being trans is out of their control. Nevertheless, the foundation of transness as a medical condition can be problematic, because it can lead people to treat trans people differently. It also treats being trans as a problem that needs to be solved by medical professionals, which takes personal autonomy away from the person transitioning. We'll cover these topics in detail in each of the following sections.

"Nobody asks cisgender people what made them the way they are. To me, gender comes from many places, from nature and from nurture, and all we [really] need to know is that some people function better in the world if they are allowed to transition, so accepting and celebrating that can only be a good thing." (Ricky)

An alternative view of gender

An alternative view of gender is that it is purely a social construct. When babies are born, they are raised in a society that sets rules about their behaviour, their hobbies, their interests and their futures and establishes all sorts of other expectations that the child needs to live up to based purely on the gender they were assigned at birth. Even if the parents actively work to avoid placing these burdens on their children, as soon as the children come into contact with the wider world (such as when they go to school), these expectations are often forced on them by not just their teachers but also their peers.

An example of the long-term impact of gendering can be seen in the number of women who are involved in computer science. In the history of computing, a lot of computing pioneers were women; for example, Ada Lovelace was the first computer programmer in the 1800s, but in the 1980s, the number of women who studied computer science started to drop dramatically. The reason for the sharp drop? The advent of the personal computer. The first personal computers were advertised and marketed specifically to boys and men. It wasn't necessarily the idea that the personal computer was not being bought by or for girls that led to this sharp decline; the actual problem is that the marketing started a narrative that computing isn't for girls. This idea that girls aren't interested in computer science or aren't very good at it is still a problem today.

This enforced social construct of gender becomes important when looking at trans issues. The sense that a person doesn't fit with what's expected of them based on their assigned gender can cause a lot of distress for the person; the idea is that they are letting the side down. This doesn't invalidate trans people or what they go through; in fact, it shows just how difficult it is to navigate a world where gender rules are enforced from such a young age (think of the trend of gender reveal parties, which actually impose the gender rules on a child before they are even born).

"I've had people say to me that gender is a social construct, that people should be able to wear what they like and feel free not to conform to gender stereotypes, so why the need to change gender? I tell them that I do agree, sort of. I think gender expression is heavily influenced by societal norms [and] the rules that we blindly follow that tell us who can wear what and which roles are considered acceptable for men and women are man-made and on the whole utterly arbitrary. But a person's gender is innate within them; it's built into the wiring of their brain [and] it's who they are. This isn't something you get to choose; you don't wake up one day and decide." (Helen)

The medical model

"To be honest, from my perspective, I don't know where [being trans] comes from, but there must be something wrong in the chemical and genetic makeup of the individuals." (Avril)

The medical model assumes that being trans is a problem that can be fixed with the correct treatment. I use these terms loosely, because there is a fundamental issue with viewing being trans through this specific lens. It means that anyone who isn't trans (who is cisgender) is seen as normal. It also means that rather than viewing all trans people as individuals, the medical model assumes there is a single way to treat trans people and that, once they have been treated, they are no longer trans.

"My wife actually feels that she was a cis man once, but 'I grew out of it.' So she's a counter-example to the idea that transness is inherent or present from birth. Neither of us has a good idea of what causes it, but we're both in agreement that it doesn't matter; the treatment is the same, regardless of the cause (transition options should be available and trans people should be treated with respect)." (Tasha Martin)

An unintended consequence of this is that being trans can be seen as abnormal and perhaps even something that can be cured or possibly prevented.

"What is trans and where does it come from? As the author says, on [the] one hand it shouldn't matter, but on [the] other, how we feel about it can be a big deal. I make sense of it using a medicalised explanation which sees it as being like many other disabilities which occur in the womb. My husband, however, whilst agreeing that there is probably some biological cause involved, finds the explanation of disability really difficult.

I was scared that he would never understand how I felt about it. I was supportive, but I was supportive because I saw it as being like a disability. The transition was to me about fixing something that had gone wrong. I know this annoyed him because he doesn't see it like that, but it is the only way that I can understand it. For me, it is the only explanation which means there is absolutely no choice involved in this, and as I see it, there is no choice. Transitioning and the chemicals and surgery involved have saved his life.

The only issue I have with this explanation is that I know it does not so neatly fit non-binary genderqueer [people] (which my sibling happens to be)." (Sally Rush)

The medical model doesn't allow us to celebrate gender diversity, it doesn't allow us to see trans people as normal, and it can be very harmful by not allowing trans people to determine their own paths without being subjected to the bureaucracy involved in medical interventions.

Can being trans be cured?

No.

In terms of the above differences between gender and sex, it is also important to clarify that being trans cannot be "cured". Although some trans people wait years before seeking treatment (for various reasons), being trans isn't something that will go away or that someone can be talked out of. There is no such thing as "if you loved me, you wouldn't be trans"; that's a terrible position to put both yourself and your partner in, because you'll feel betrayed that they continue to be trans and they will feel betrayed that you want them to be someone that they aren't. Even the UK medical profession has agreed in the Memorandum of Understanding on Conversion Therapy that gender identity cannot be cured.[1]

Conversion therapy is the practice of using psychotherapy and other means to reduce or stop same-sex attraction and or alter gender identity and is firmly rooted in the belief that being trans (or lesbian, bisexual or gay) is a mental illness that can be cured. These therapies have been shown to be unethical and harmful, and ultimately they don't work.

In 2017, gender was added to the Memorandum of Understanding on Conversion Therapy (Stonewall, 2016) that was signed by a number of key bodies:

- The Association of LGBT Doctors and Dentists

---

[1] See www.psychotherapy.org.uk/wp-content/uploads/2016/09/Memorandum-of-understanding-on-conversion-therapy.pdf

- British Association for Behavioural and Cognitive Psychotherapies
- British Association for Counselling and Psychotherapy
- British Psychoanalytic Council
- The British Psychological Society
- College of Sexual and Relationship Therapists
- The National Counselling Society
- NHS Scotland
- Pink Therapy
- Royal College of General Practitioners
- Scottish Government
- Stonewall
- UK Council for Psychotherapy.

By signing this memorandum of understanding, these organisations have agreed that no members will carry out or advocate conversion therapy for trans, bisexual, lesbian or gay people.

Preference and transphobia

Just as a sidebar, it's also helpful to think about the difference between sexual preference and transphobia. If you're reading the book, you may already know this, but it's an important thought process to work through.

It's helpful to get past the idea of sex always being about genitals. Trans people have complicated relationships with their genitals, and many trans people wouldn't use their parts in a heteronormative way (that's a little bit like assuming that two women can't have sex because there isn't a penis). It's also important not to assume that a trans woman has a penis (or a trans man has a vagina) in the first place, as that can be the core of the problem.

I'm not arguing that it is a problem if you see someone across the room and you're just not into them. Maybe you don't like tall women or short ones or trans ones. That's completely fine. It's your choice, and you're completely entitled to it. Some people just aren't attracted to some other people. There's no judgment there.

Where the problem comes in is on a personal level: that is, if you meet someone and you think they are wonderful and smart and sexy and all that sort of stuff and you get to the point where you're deciding to have sex (for example, as part of a discussion of what you're into), and then the person tells you that they are trans. If, at that point, you think the idea of sex is now icky, you need to think about what assumptions you are making and why that is, because it is probably rooted in transphobia.

There is a common trope that is put out by the media that trans people are out to deceive people, especially to deceive people into having sex with them. The reality is that, for many single trans people, the dilemma of when to tell is a really hard one. If you tell really early, then you risk the person not getting to know you first (because of their innate prejudices), and if you tell them later, you risk being seen as a deceiver.

Imagine you had a large birthmark on your privates, something that meant that you were almost guaranteed to be rejected, and imagine a society where repulsion at birthmarks was both a common trope in comedy and potentially could get you killed if people found out. At what stage would you tell?

I think that once you've tried it out with someone and aren't into it, that's cool. Chemistry doesn't work out for everyone. There could be a host of reasons why it doesn't work out once you've tried, but to me, not trying at all with someone who was attractive mere minutes before is the bit that becomes problematic.

As a trans person, walking away when you find out someone is trans sends a strong message that this is because of transphobia. It's saying "Look, I have all these assumptions about what a trans person is and what sex may be like. While you are good enough for me to be attracted to, when it comes down to it, I'm out."

Equality Act 2010

It's important to touch on the Equality Act 2010 in the UK, especially with regards to trans people and partnerships. The Equality Act 2010 replaced a number of different pieces of legislation that covered discrimination and was aimed specifically at simplifying the law.

The Act rendered it against the law to discriminate against people based on a number of protected characteristics, which are:

- age
- disability
- gender reassignment
- marriage and civil partnership
- pregnancy and maternity
- race
- religion or belief
- sex
- sexual orientation.

The wording may not be ideal, but trans people are covered under "gender reassignment", which is specifically defined as "a person has proposed, started or completed a process to change his or her sex…[a] transsexual person has the protected characteristic of gender reassignment" (HM Government, 2010).

This means that a person cannot be discriminated against, harassed or victimised because of any one (or combination) of the above protected characteristics, and the Act covers, amongst others, provisions for:

- shopping or services (when a person is getting a service or goods provided either by a company or by a public office)

- associations (such as private clubs and political associations)

- housing (either in renting, selling or buying a property)

- work (in employing someone, treatment at work, equal pay, pregnancy, maternity, etc., and an employer cannot ask a person about their disability or health prior to employment)

- education (both school pupils and students and applicants to education)

- third parties (making it unlawful for anyone to harass, discriminate against or victimise an ex-employee or ex-pupil or to aid someone else in discriminating against that person).

If you feel that you have been discriminated against because of your relationship (or your partner has been discriminated against because they are trans), it's important to seek legal advice so that you can make a complaint.

2

Finding Out Your Partner Is Trans

Finding out that your partner is trans can be quite confusing for people, and the responses can vary greatly depending on loads of different factors. The first factor is how far into the relationship you discover this.

For people who know their partner is trans before they get together, managing transition and their identity as a partner of a trans person can be easier.

"I found out when my wife and I got together. She was still living as a man and spent most of the evening trying to convince me that her being trans was a reason for us to not be together. She felt that being trans meant that she could never be in a successful relationship because her transness would always get in the way. I, of course, spent most of the evening convincing her that she was worthy of love and that we could make it work together. To be completely honest, I had no idea what being trans meant, other than being a huge fan of the *Rocky Horror Picture Show* when I was a teenager (I now recognise how massively problematic *Rocky Horror* is for many people). I sometimes think that it was this fact, asserting that trans people deserve love just like everyone else without any idea what the practicalities would be, that kept us together. No matter how hard things got, no matter what we went through, it always came back down to the fact that she is deserving of love, and I took it upon myself to prove to her that I was right about that." (Jo)

That being said, there are still challenges for people who know beforehand, because there is an expectation that they will know how to manage their feelings as their partner transitions.

"But that doesn't mean that it's easy. It was difficult. I felt completely out of my depth. There were times when I didn't understand why she was the way that she was. I didn't get how anyone could just know anything so completely and be so stubborn about it. There were times that it was lonely and times when I couldn't talk to anyone for fear of having them judge her and by association me. There were times where I would go to functions on my own because she didn't want to be on display. It was hard, and I'm not going to deny it. But it does get better. It gets easier, and you get stronger." (Jo)

There are also times when you find out that your partner is trans but are still unprepared for what to expect in the long run.

"My partner and I had been friends for a while before she told me. At the time, she was very confused about it and linked it more with her sexuality rather than her gender identity. Our relationship developed beyond friendship. While she mentioned it occasionally and dressed up in women's clothing, she never talked about transitioning, and we both seemed content with the odd 'role-play' session. Around the time she got a new job, she began to get depressed, so I encouraged her to visit a therapist (as she did during her teenage years). The therapist suggested a more regular outing in her female form (one weekend a month), which we trialled. Five weeks before our wedding, she told me that she wanted to transition into a woman full time, and [she] did so within two weeks of us getting married. People ask me why we still got married when I knew she was going to transition, but, to me, she was the same person I had fallen in love with – it didn't matter what she wore. When she applied for her GRC [Gender Recognition Certificate], I had to sign a form to state that we wanted to remain married after her gender was officially changed to female, which I was happy to sign." (Stevie)

Finding out that your partner is trans once you've been together for a while (be that a few months or a few years) can be difficult because so much of your identity is tied to the relationship and the history that you share.

"'A few months ago I was looking through some old photos and came across one of my husband looking incredibly young, proudly holding our newborn first baby. I smiled fondly at the memory but then felt incredibly sad as I remembered the sweet, caring, sensitive boy I had met and fallen head over heels in love with. Fifteen years of depression, a job he hates, and three more babies later, that boy is little more than a memory. I still love the man he is, but I have wished for many years that I had the ability to make things better for him, to lift the weight of his depression, and in that moment it hit me suddenly and painfully just how much the years had changed him.' I wrote that nearly three years ago, not long after my partner first told me she was trans. [R]eading it now it feels so strange, [and] the use of 'he' throughout seems wrong. I'm married to a woman now, and in truth I always was; this is how I realised that...

So, it all started for me with a pair of fleecy tights; sounds crazy, but it's true! I'd just picked up a pair from a local shop and suggested that she might want a pair. I was thinking on a purely practical level of how cosy and warm they were, so good for wearing under jeans for doing outdoor stuff in the cold weather. There was just something in the way she reacted to the suggestion and how she rushed straight off to get them and try them out that made me pause and ask 'You do just want these to keep warm, don't you?' I'm not sure I even knew what I was really asking. I guess I knew there was something more than the depression going on with her, as about seven years ago when I worked shifts that finished at midnight, I came home once to find her wearing a pair of my black lacy knickers. She managed to convince me that it was just a one-off, trying it out on a whim type thing, and I didn't really give it another thought for a long time. Fairly recently, she had told me that when she was about 12 years old, she had wished that she could magically wake up one day as a girl. She put this down to the bullying she was subjected to throughout school; the theory being that the bullies would leave her alone if she was a girl, and that sounded completely plausible. The memory of the lacy knickers jumped back into my mind on hearing this, but at no point had the idea that she could be trans crossed my mind.

It seems so obvious now, but up to that point, it wasn't. That said, I wasn't shocked, surprised perhaps, but the more we talked, the more sense it all made. Whilst I was fine with the idea in theory when she suggested trying on some of my clothes, I was scared that I would react wrongly (do or say something to make her feel embarrassed or uncomfortable). I had butterflies in my tummy as she got changed; all sorts of thoughts were going through my head. What if I freaked out? Surely I should be finding this whole idea weirder than I was; maybe I was just suppressing my feelings and they would all burst out of me when I saw her dressed as a her! I looked up, and none of those things happened. I just saw the person I loved; okay, she was wearing my clothes, but hey, it's only social conditioning that tells me that boys can't wear skirts anyway (not sure the same applies to the fake boobs, but you know what I mean). Not only was I not freaked out by this new side of my husband, but I quickly came to realise that something magical happened when she put my clothes on: she talked about feelings. I found out for the first time in years what was going on inside her head, and I rather liked it.

It was a little like opening the floodgates, hardly surprising when this girl living inside had been squashed in a box for 30 years, and I had lots of chances over the next couple of weeks to meet her. She would change clothes and instantly was different; it was as if her entire being was giving a sigh of relief when she became her real self. I began to feel positive about the future. I had no idea where this was going to take us, but it quickly seemed obvious that the depression was very likely to be linked to the fact that she had been living a lie her entire life, trying to be something she wasn't, [and] I felt there was hope.

But that's not the best bit; no, the best bit is that I suddenly realised that I already knew the girl living inside my husband. Remember the sweet, caring, sensitive boy I had met and fallen head over heels in love with? Turns out she was a sweet, caring, sensitive girl, and now I get to spend my life with her.

Life doesn't always pan out the way that you expect, and I certainly didn't expect this, but she is so much happier now, and I am too. We are moving toward a better, happier life." (Helen)

The key, though, is communication. You'll see that I keep repeating that. I cannot stress enough how important it is for you to talk about not just what your partner is going through and what they want but also what you're going through and what you want.

"We first started seeing each other when he identified as lesbian, before any mention of being transgender. As far as I was aware, he had always identified as lesbian, apart from a few years ago [when] he got into a rather destructive S&M relationship where he packed and lived as male. Not knowing much about transgenderism at the time, I just thought this was a sexual thing within that relationship and didn't question it. I knew he would tell me anything he needed me to know in his own time. Ours was a volatile relationship due to a lack of communication, and he was experiencing some mental health issues (diagnosed with borderline personality disorder) as well as coping with his gender dysphoria. I didn't know this at the time and just thought he was being selfish and self-destructive. We split up, became friends, argued, got back together, split up, became friends again, and this time it stuck, because we were honest with each other and [about] what we wanted from life." (Rene)

No matter when you find out, though, the crucial thing is that you need to go through transition together. As your partner changes, your relationship will change, and so will your individual identity.

"Facing transition together is what helped; me being there for her, talking to her and supporting her helped. She talked to me about what she was feeling, what she was going through, what her next steps would be and what her hopes and fears were. I spoke to her too, about what I was afraid of, what I was hoping for and what I was losing. Together we made it, though, and I honestly think we are both better people for it. We certainly are both much happier." (Jo)

There are some things that we need to talk about when it comes to the very start of the whole process, and a lot of these are the hugely harmful stereotypes and narratives that exist.

"When my husband came out to me, it took me by surprise. We had been discussing his gender identity for a relatively small amount of time, and he until then believed he might [have] been genderfluid. In my ignorance, I thought all that would change was his clothing choices, but he never dressed 'girly' anyway. He only wore a dress at our wedding four months prior due to society and family pressure that girls wear dresses at their weddings. He hated it and wanted to take it off as soon as we got to the reception.

I spent about a week either crying or close to crying. I felt that everything was going to change, that 'she' would be different, [and] that I was going to lose my 'wife'. I felt like our four-year relationship and four months of marriage was a lie, that something was hidden from me, even though he hadn't realised his feelings until recently.

I had then realised there were signs in my relationship that I had missed, but it was then that I realised my 'wife' was still the same person and would still be the same person. All that would change was his body. The heart of the person I fell in love with was still the same." (Anne)

Disclosure

A partner coming out to you as trans or even saying that they think they may be trans can be one of the hardest things as a partner. Living with a secret that doesn't belong to you can be very difficult for partners, because you may feel like you cannot speak to anyone else about what you and your partner are going through without betraying your partner's trust.

"I met my partner 12 years ago. My partner was then female and identified as a lesbian. We met via friends whilst he had been visiting family in the UK. As [he was] a South African national, time was limited, and our relationship was very new when immigration detained him for overstaying his visa and subsequently chucked him out of the country. We then spent ten long months apart whilst fighting for a visa back into the UK. I visited him twice out in South Africa; however, most of our relationship was based on long telephone conversations throughout this period. After three failed attempts at getting a visa, we eventually obtained the first 'same-sex' visa once the law changed here in the UK in regards to same-sex marriage. We were ecstatic, and my partner came to live with me and my two teenage sons. My family were welcoming and happy to see how happy I was at last. I was the main breadwinner and worked full time as a senior social worker. It was strange to be living with someone who I barely dated before our long distance relationship flourished. It was an exciting time in our lives, and we held our civil partnership ceremony in a castle in the midst of the Brecon mountains of Wales. It was the most beautiful day in the most beautiful surroundings. My family and our friends joined us, and everyone agreed it was the happiest wedding they had attended.

The next couple of years were the happiest I had ever been, even though financially we were struggling initially. However, things settled, we bought our own home, and both our careers flourished. During the first five years of marriage, my partner never mentioned the dilemma he was feeling. It was something that didn't appear to be problematic, and I was happy with how our relationship revolved around respect and love. I'm not exactly sure when my partner brought it up, but the first time the transgender topic was mentioned, I was clear in my response that 'if I had wanted to be married to a man, I would have married a man'. The negativity of my response ended the discussion, but it played on my mind for a while afterwards. In February 2011, I became ill and could no longer work. My partner became my fulltime carer and had to give up work to look after me. The relationship was under a great pressure financially and emotionally whilst we both came to terms with the realisation that our roles had reversed and I was no longer an independent person.

During this time, we watched several documentaries on transgender individuals, and we had lots of conversations, and it clearly was an issue for my partner. I had time to explore my feelings and acknowledged it was something my partner was struggling with, but the fear of our relationship ending and my previous remark had made the topic difficult for him to approach again with me. Becoming ill had highlighted that our relationship was based on love and respect, and my sexuality became secondary. After an openhearted discussion on our fear of me dying [and] the issue of ensuring both of us would remain happy, my partner brought up his wish to become the man he felt he should have been all along. Eventually, my partner spoke to his GP, and the ball started rolling." (Nicola Kalisky)

It is important that, as a partner, you recognise that the secret is not yours. It may be difficult that you aren't able to talk to anyone else about what is going on, but you need to make sure that you respect your partner's wishes. Some people would prefer not to tell anyone until they have worked through the issues for themselves, while others are comfortable with it being shared with friends and family. Either way, it's vital that you don't share the information with anyone else unless the trans person has consented.

"When I first realised my husband was trans, he had been repressing it for years and was terrified I was going to reject him. We happened to be in bed, and I had made a comment I thought was funny, but it made him turn his back on me, the sign I had hit a really raw nerve. We discussed what was going on, and over a short period after that initial coming out, there was a more complete coming out.

It's been a scary journey, especially in the early stages. I didn't really understand what was going on and was scared. I was scared about what the person I loved was saying. Even though I had identified – before he said anything – something of what was going on, it messed with my head. I live in a world when it's much easier to think in terms of the binary (i.e. male and female).

I was scared by how scared he was. There were a lot of tears, and I knew he was really hurting inside. I also had an awareness that a lot of trans people end up taking their own lives, and that scared me lots. I was worried that he wouldn't make it through.

I was scared about how other people would react to him. He had talked about fears of being attacked, and that got me really scared. As time went on, that fear subsided, but I was upset that he got aggro, especially one morning when he went to the loo in a coffee shop. This was overcome a bit when we worked out where had the gender-neutral toilets and were able to plan things like where we did coffee around this." (Sally Rush)

While you can feel like you have no one to talk to, remember that you have your partner. You have the opportunity to work things out together; it can be a very emotional and terrifying time for you, but if your partner has just come out to you, you may find that they are just as scared as you are.

"I have known my partner for a long time, long before we ever had a romantic relationship. We were friends, and I was still married to my husband at the time. My partner was in college, and we regularly wrote letters and spoke on the phone. One day, during one of our conversations, he came out to me as trans. He told me that he identified as male and explained that he had always felt that way. I have to say, I wasn't at all surprised. He presented as fairly androgynous and identified as queer/lesbian when we first met. Though I didn't know it at the time, he went to great lengths to minimise his more feminine features. I think we are somewhat unusual, because we weren't in a romantic relationship – that didn't happen until many years later. I was happy for him and wanted to support his exploration of who he was and what it meant. After our phone call, I even sat down with my children, who were six, seven and eight at the time, and explained it to them, and while he wasn't out to everyone else in his life, we have used his preferred pronouns for the past 16 years." (Julia)

For trans people to disclose their trans identity can be very complicated; on the one hand, they want to be seen as just people and judged purely on who they are, but on the other hand, not disclosing can be dangerous when the person they're with finds out. Of course, the flip side to this is that if they disclose, they run the risk of people not being interested (because there is such a stigma against trans people) or people seeing them as a curiosity.

"We met online, on an asexual friendship and dating site, and it was written on his profile that he was a stealth trans guy. I hadn't met a trans person before, but I also didn't think anything of it. As someone who has only been attracted to males, I didn't see him [as] any different than a cis guy." (Shae)

The other issue is that a person's trans identity is a hugely complex and personal thing. Disclosing a full medical or family history isn't necessary for cis people, whereas some people somehow feel that they have a right to know this about trans people from the start. It can be especially complicated when you are in the queer community and meet someone whose friends know that they are trans.

"I found out my partner was trans from another trans friend who was attending the same support group as him. My partner was very angry at first about the breach of confidentiality, but in the end we three managed to negotiate round this. At the time, we had not yet entered into a relationship but were just at the 'having coffee' phase. I was disappointed to find out that he was not a woman, so

I suppose that should have been a sign, really. However, as I am attracted to people of various genders, I hoped that if we stayed communicating, it would be something we could go through together, and [I] continued into the relationship on that basis." (Sasha)

When you find out your partner is trans, it's important to seek out support groups, either online or in person. Some gender clinics have started offering services to partners of trans people, but there is also a wealth of information online.

The myth of always knowing

A common narrative portrayed in the media is that trans people have always known that they were trans. The common phrase "born in the wrong body" can create an illusion that all trans people know from a very young age that they are trans and thus spend their lives deceiving people.

"My wife didn't figure it out herself until she was 31; she did tell me within a week of realising that she needed to do something about this (and she spent that week agonising). It was just before our ninth wedding anniversary, and I was shocked and definitely scared. I was bisexual, so I knew I would be willing to present myself as being in a lesbian marriage, but I also realised there were going to be all sorts of terrifying and sometimes unexpected changes. She tried briefly to 'just cross-dress' or to maintain that she wouldn't 'fully transition', but I think we both suspected fairly quickly that she was in denial." (Tasha Martin)

The danger of the always knowing myth is that it can create a barrier between the trans person and their partner. It relies on the idea that a trans person has knowingly entered the relationship and tricked the other party into getting involved with them. It breaks down the trust within the relationship and can leave partners feeling betrayed, resentful, angry, hurt and abandoned.

> "Of course, she came out to me by giving me a book to read in which the trans woman ends up in a platonic relationship with her wife after their marriage is effectively destroyed. As a note to anyone thinking of ways to drop this bomb, do *not* do that! I thought she was trying to tell me that she saw no hope for our romantic relationship, and I was so upset and confused that I didn't try to straighten out that misconception for several horrible weeks. In reality, she'd tried to find the best book about trans people that she could, and it just wasn't very good. Once we started really talking again (and we've based our entire friendship and marriage on talking), we figured out that we were both committed to making this work." (Tasha Martin)

As society becomes more accepting of trans people, the narrative is changing. The language is evolving to a point where people are better able to explain what they actually mean when they say they've always known.

> "I didn't feel betrayed or lied to, though. We'd been together since we were 17 years old, so whatever clues there were about her gender identity before this, I had access to the information too. Neither of us suspected a thing, but I knew she hadn't been hiding things from me." (Tasha Martin)

I think that it's more helpful to think of it as a person knowing that something is different and they don't feel like other people but only much later getting to the realisation that they may be trans. This, to me, is where the difference between dysphoria and the trans identity comes in. A person can have gender dysphoria but not understand what it is or how to deal with it for a long time before reaching the point where, through some circumstance (for example, counselling, searching online or meeting another trans person), they actually come to the realisation that they may be trans. Realising that they may be trans is also not the same as embracing the identity. Some people will identify as trans and not want to transition or change their bodies; some trans people will feel an urgent need to transition because there is a sense of feeling like they've wasted so much time; and there are many other points along that continuum.

> "Whilst I did not feel that there had been a deception, I know many partners of trans people do feel this. I think the extent to which this is the case often depends upon the age at which the trans person comes out. As my partner and I had been together a relatively short time in the scheme of things and he was quite young, it was a very different situation to [what] those who have been together decades face. Additionally, the coming out to me occurred when I realised something was being repressed. Therefore, I felt more sadness than deception. Many older people (particularly if their partners do come out when children have left home or they have retired) do feel similar feelings of deception to those who find out their partners have had an affair." (Sally Rush)

Recognising that you are trans is separate from dealing with dysphoria. I think it's important to distinguish the two. But the myth will continue as long as there is a persistent need for a trans person to defend their identity, to explain that it's not their fault, or to conform to the standard narrative in order to get medical interventions.

The myth of divorce as a prerequisite to transition

One of the myths that people face is that trans people need to get a divorce in order to transition. Frustratingly, this myth is still relatively common, especially with the trans narratives of public figures such as Kelly Malone and Caitlyn Jenner. It's also generally more commonly assumed of trans women.

The myth can often make partners feel like their feelings are being disregarded or they are being thrown to the curb in order for the trans person to follow their dreams. This, of course, may happen in some cases, but it is definitely not a prerequisite to transition.

> "It was important to talk through every step of the transition and identify feelings along the way. My partner became obsessed with researching. Although [it was] difficult sometimes, it was important for him to do this, as he had not been able to truly explore the steps he would need to take and chat to others who were further along the process. I did find I got angry at times with the lack of support for partners and the whole world revolving around the transition. Usually, the anger led to tears of mourning our same-sex relationship and redefining us individually within the journey." (Nicola Kalisky)

In a survey carried out by the National Center for Transgender Equality and the National LGBTQ Task Force in 2008 (Tanis *et al.*, 2011), only 45 per cent of those trans people who came out to partners had those relationships end.

That statistic may look like a lot, but when you compare it to the divorce rates in the general population of 47 per cent (53% in the United States) it's actually pretty standard. It does also mean that 55 per cent of relationships didn't end when a person came out as trans.

When looking more closely at the data, it becomes clear that those 45 per cent of relationships ended for people who had completed transition (that means that the relationship ended some time during transition). This is also related to gender and age; trans women's relationships end more frequently than those of trans men, and the older a person is, the more likely the relationship will end.

While these statistics look really scary, remember that for all the ones that ended, there are a lot that do survive. Transition is tough, but it's worth it to at least give the relationship a chance of surviving.

"The prevalence of the myth that we need to divorce in order to transition terrified me. I thought that for her to be able to transition, we would have to dissolve the relationship. My wife didn't want transition to cause our relationship to fail, so we kept talking. At every stage throughout transition, we'd be checking in with each other to make sure we still wanted to be together, and we did (and still do). I wanted to be there for her and help her through as much as I could, but I also wanted to make sure that we were okay. I selfishly wanted to be with her; I didn't want to give her up.

One of the most helpful pieces of advice I had was to take it one day at a time. Every day, I would ask myself if I still wanted to be in a relationship with her, and as each stage brought her closer and closer to who she wanted to be, I found that I actually wanted to be with her more. As each stage of transition progressed, she became happier in her skin, which meant that we were happier as a couple. It's now many years later, and we're still happy. I still remember that advice, though, and I now use it in all sorts of aspects of my life. Every day, I check in to see if I'm still happy at work, and if not, I start making changes to get myself closer to who I want to be. In a way, supporting my wife through her transition actually helped me to be a better, happier, more whole, more happy person." (Jo)

There is, of course, a small kernel of truth within the myth. In the UK, if your partner goes through a legal transition and changes their birth certificate by applying for a Gender Recognition Certificate (GRC), you will need to give spousal consent for the marriage to continue (and if you're in a civil partnership, the partnership will need to be dissolved and converted into a marriage).

"With regard to the myth around divorce, it is one of the many which do the rounds. However, if you are in a civil partnership and your partner transitions, you will have to convert to marriage in order for them to get their GRC. This was something I found really difficult." (Sally Rush)

Splitting up for transition

Some couples think that in order for there to be the least disruption to the family, they should live apart for all or part of transition. While I cannot advocate anything other than what works for you in a relationship, there are some serious cautions I can offer from experience with working with partners. Of course, this doesn't apply if you aren't living together before transition, although you may want to look at some of the considerations and put plans in place to ensure you don't get tripped up by them.

Deciding to transition while in a relationship can be one of the hardest things a trans person can face. Because of all the myths surrounding relationship with trans people, they sometimes believe that they are unlovable and will need to break up the relationship before transitioning. Telling you that they are trans is one of the most authentic things your partner can do, which leaves them feeling extremely vulnerable. If you decide, even for very rational reasons, that you should be apart while they transition, there is an underlying message that may make your partner feel like they are being rejected. This rejection will ultimately harm your relationship, if it does survive transition at all.

The reason that the relationship may fail when you are apart is not due to transition or even the rejection that the trans person may feel but may be due to the separation itself. In separating from the relationship during transition, you are also removing a key support system, not just for the trans person but also yourself. No one other than the people in the relationship knows what it means to them, and no one else understands what the impact of transition is on you both as individuals and as a couple.

There is also a very practical reason to be physically in the same space together, and that is because your partner is bound to change during transition, sometimes in small ways and sometimes in bigger ones. If you are apart, that can make those changes more dramatic and much harder for you to deal with. As the changes happen, your partner will be more and more pleased and will be looking for your approval and support. If you haven't had time to adjust to the changes gradually, these changes can come as a shock, which can leave you unprepared to respond. In addition, the language and culture of being trans can be quite confusing (especially because the language is evolving quickly), and using the wrong words can be hurtful to a sensitive trans person.

> "I was scared that because I was gay, I wouldn't be able to stay with him when he transitioned, and if we did, things would never be the same in the bedroom. Then I was scared about the impact of surgery and if it would all go okay. I was scared about how you talk about it and when. I was scared that the church might reject us both, and I was scared that his employers might not be great. I was scared it might damage what felt like a fragile relationship with his parents.
>
> There was a lot of fear around, as you can see. But as my journey has gone on, my journey, our journey, has felt a lot different [than] expected. Where I expected him to face rejection by the church and work, he has on the whole experienced love. That's not to say there haven't been people who have used the Bible to be transphobic, but on the whole there has been love. People tend to be much more loving and understanding than we often give them credit for.

Where I expected our relationship to fall apart, it nearly did, but we got through that largely by hugs. We found a way to talk about things...somehow...and we cried lots, but we didn't let this destroy us. Where I expected him to fall apart, he actually began to blossom. As he stopped repressing things, he actually became a much happier person, and that made life easier." (Sally Rush)

Transition is a time when you and your partner are both building identities; if you aren't around, you may find that you drift apart from them and it gets more and more difficult to be together. When your partner transitions, you will both be different as a result of that in the same way that winning the lottery can change a relationship. I will always advocate choosing to stay, battling out the hard times together, and being there for the joys, the little celebrations and the small mercies.

Pronouns

As early as possible, trans people will start using their correct pronouns, so I'm going to explore what pronouns are and how to tackle the whole topic. As an aside, I have specifically avoided the term "preferred pronoun", because the pronoun that a person asks you to use for them should not be seen as that person's preference. It is the correct pronoun for their gender (irrespective of their gender assigned at birth).

Pronouns are the words we use to refer to someone instead of using their name. The common masculine ones are "he/ him/his", and the common feminine ones are "she/her/hers". Non-binary pronouns are entirely dependent on the individual, but the most commonly used non-binary pronouns are the singular "they/their/theirs". Some people choose to have no pronouns at all and will ask people to just use their name, while others request "ze/hir/hirs". There are many new emerging pronouns, and it is always the prerogative of the trans person to specify what pronoun should be used for them.

Getting used to pronouns can be very complicated, especially for people who are in a relationship with someone when the pronouns change. It can be difficult to adjust, and that difficulty can also be further compounded by the fact that in some contexts the trans person isn't out yet, which means changing the pronouns to fit the circumstance. It's important to remember that, for many trans people, coming out can cause a huge sense of anxiety, and using their pronouns (even if initially just in private) can be a powerful way to show them that you support them.

"The first time I felt what it was like for my partner to be misgendered was after our first-ever Brighton Trans Pride. He was still a 'very butch' lesbian then, and I knew in my heart that he was trans something, though he had never fully voiced it. At Trans Pride, he was the most physically relaxed I had seen him and the most affectionate he had ever been in public. He just sort of uncoiled, let go of a long-held breath and was, for a shy introvert who doesn't like crowds, the most comfortable I'd seen him in our six-month relationship. Afterwards, we went for food, and our very nice waitress brought us our drinks and said 'there you go ladies', and I felt for the first time [that] '*No*', that's not right. It was a prickly feeling, and a wrong incompleteness, a bit like that sensation where you *know* you didn't eat all your biscuit but can't find the rest of it. At the same time, I felt him instantly curl in on himself and coil back up. Two and a half years on since coming out and being regularly correctly gendered, he has blossomed more than I could ever imagine. If he is misgendered and I'm around, it still jars, but I just do a correct-pronoun-heavy sentence straight afterwards. Even though I struggled at first going from she to he, it's now so natural that when someone slips up and says 'where's she gone?', my first thought is 'who?!'" (Josephine Humphrey)

Misgendering is when a person uses the wrong pronouns for a person, usually by applying the pronouns that match the gender that was assigned at birth instead of the pronouns that match their gender identity. It is vitally important that if you do get a pronoun wrong, you apologise and move on quickly. If you make a big deal of getting it wrong, you are only serving to make the trans person feel even more uncomfortable than the original misgendering would have (especially if it is couched in explanations of how they appear).

Misgendering can be a simple mistake, but it can also be used as a way to bully a trans person. This is especially true when trans people are out in public, and it is often used as a way for a transphobic person to provoke a reaction by a trans person. If you are with your partner and they get misgendered, make sure you look after your partner first. Acknowledge what has happened and ask them what they would like you to do to help. If they say they don't want you to do anything, then it is better to do nothing and walk away. You may feel the urge to step in and be protective, but this can make the situation worse by provoking a confrontation that may make the trans person feel even more uncomfortable or even put you both in danger.

3

Gender Dysphoria

The key to understanding what being trans is actually about is the understanding of the concept of gender dysphoria. Gender dysphoria is a sense of unease or distress with a person's gender, and it can manifest in very different ways, which makes it difficult to define and describe.

> "I don't have enough personal experience to speak about dysphoria, though I am a witness. I think, in terms of managing their dysphoria, the best we can do as partners or loved ones is try to just be as accepting as possible and work to be especially conscious of pronouns." (Julia)

At its core, gender dysphoria is a feeling of dissatisfaction associated with a mismatch between a person's gender which was assigned at birth (also *sex*) and their gender identity.

> "This generally is a negative thing [related to] the severe unhappiness and depression of having a body which does not match the inside. It is very difficult to deal with a partner who is suffering the negative feelings surrounding this. I always try to be positive, as my partner manages very well in finding all the negatives! I think communicating has to be the top tip. Sometimes, the trans partner does not always confide their inner feelings, and even though we are 15 years down the line, she still says things that I am unaware of or didn't know. I think that being a partner,

though, it is also important not to lose sight of who you are, as the trans thing can take over your whole life. If the trans partner decides to medicate (self- or otherwise), this does help with the dysphoria, as their body does start to change. Even without medication, it can be the small things that can make a difference; MTF [male-to-female] eyebrows being 'on point', manicured nails, etc. Also, no secrets... You need to be honest with each other." (Avril)

In individuals, this manifests as either what I call social gender dysphoria or physical gender dysphoria.

Social gender dysphoria

Social dysphoria can occur when people are required to do tasks that are associated with gender roles that do not fit their gender identity, and it can vary between cultures and even upbringings. This can manifest in different ways; to illustrate the point, some trans women will experience social dysphoria when doing things that are traditionally male, such as taking out the bins or doing the gardening, and some trans men will experience social dysphoria when doing traditionally female tasks such as the washing up or cleaning the house. For all trans people, especially non-binary people, social dysphoria varies based on an individual's views. Thus some non-binary people will continue to do tasks that are traditionally associated with their assigned gender while also taking on tasks that are associated with the opposite gender. This social dysphoria can also change over time and may manifest itself as more or less of an issue based on how comfortable a trans person is in their gender identity.

For cis people, these small transgressions of gender norms are seen as acceptable, and in some areas, it is actually celebrated as progress (for example, cis women taking part in combat sports or cis men becoming stay-at-home parents). In these examples, I have deliberately chosen small mundane tasks that are not specifically gendered in and of themselves, because as partners we can make small changes that can have a great impact on the well-being of trans people. Renegotiating the household chores is one of the ways to do this, and compromise can be key when entering into these role negotiations. The mundaneness of the tasks also highlights how much of a double standard there is when people are judging trans people. A cis woman who doesn't wear dresses is seen as having a preference that is completely acceptable, whereas a trans woman in the same situation may be judged as not being trans enough. This disparity can be at the root of social dysphoria for some people.

This social gender dysphoria does also present in more significant and dramatic ways when outside of the realms of the home. How trans people are viewed by others can greatly impact the dysphoria that some people face. This is expertly summed up as "I'm not trapped in my body. I'm trapped in other people's perceptions of my body." When trans people are newly coming out, they can be very sensitive to how other people see them. Newly out trans people may need more validation and may choose to more explicitly express their gender identity. Some trans women will dress very femininely and completely shun any non-gendered or masculine-appearing clothing for fear of being seen as a man, and they also often wear makeup to further demonstrate their identity (for some trans women, wearing makeup could also be necessary to cover up facial hair). For trans men, the demonstration of their masculinity can lead to them acting more overtly masculine, such as being more sexually aggressive.

"What doesn't help is telling your partner it doesn't matter what people think and it doesn't matter how they look, or worse, saying they should learn to be comfortable with their bodies or they don't need to get medical treatment to be acceptable in their identity. Dysphoria, whether physical or social, is too powerful just to magic away with reassurances. We can't create an idealised bubble for our partners where trans people are accepted just as they are and don't face marginalisation, violence and stigmatisation. Their fears are not made up. My partner's fear of being mistreated by health workers or carers if his body does not all match up to expectations is justified. It took me a while to accept that it's okay for him to change his body for other people, for society, because we don't live in a perfect world. And it would be okay for him not to do that, too, but it's up to the individual what they can cope with, how prepared to stand out they are, and what they need to do to make sense of themselves and help others make sense of them. If the world does not represent an enlightened ideal around gender difference, we shouldn't have lofty expectations for trans people to challenge the status quo any more than they do by simply existing." (Ricky)

In my experience, one of the biggest triggers of social dysphoria for trans people is being misgendered. To a trans person, however far along in transition, using the wrong name or pronouns (or both) can trigger a significant bout of dysphoria. Being misgendered leads trans people to feel that no matter what they do or how far they have come, they will not be viewed as their actual gender. This is one of the key reasons why acknowledging and respecting someone's pronouns is vitally important.

Physical gender dysphoria (also referred to as body dysphoria)

Physical gender dysphoria is the negative feelings a trans person has about their body. This varies from person to person and can also vary for a given person in different situations and on different days.

"Dysphoria becomes much more acute once a trans person admits how they're feeling – what was locked down tight suddenly surfaces. That means things you used to do need to be renegotiated – every touch has to be checked out – words for things may need to change, and what you do together certainly will. Then physical changes can shift dysphoria – hormonal changes and surgery make changes to the body that can amplify the sense of incongruence about other body parts. And, of course, surgery can put a dead stop to sex during recovery, then afterwards, you are exploring something very new. A willingness to talk and experiment [and] also to be really patient with each other [is pretty essential]. The other side of things is that hormones can really change sexual feelings, and it takes a bit of time to get to grips with the new feelings – it really is like going through puberty all over again. And the clitoris grows and becomes very sensitive, which has a fun side for sure!" (Ricky)

Physical dysphoria is a feeling of wrongness that causes distress. It's often specifically with regards to the primary sex characteristics (genitals) or the secondary sex characteristics (for example, facial hair, Adam's apple, breasts, hips, weight distribution). For non-binary people, this can be particularly complicated, because they may feel physical dysphoria about their primary or secondary sex characteristics but not be able to articulate what the alternative is.

"My boyfriend was two months post-top-surgery and had been on testosterone for just over a year. At first, he didn't seem to have much dysphoria. We were quite free together, with my extreme self-consciousness being more prominent than his dysphoria. After a few months, that freedom became more restricted as his lower dysphoria started surfacing. He also has a bit of dysphoria around his chest scars and his figure that he sometimes thinks is feminine, though many cis guys have a very similar shape, and I don't think it looks remotely feminine. He's just had stage one (UK) phalloplasty and still has dysphoria that will take time to fade.

I have my own dysphoria based around my monthly cycle, as it's more on than off each month. When he gets dysphoric, he doesn't want to be looked at or touched, but when I get dysphoric, I need a lot of affection or, with my severe body image issues, intimacy would help me feel more acceptable. It was hard to adjust to our needs being so different, but we were already in love, and we had to do a lot of communicating.

Some trans people don't have any dysphoria, some have a little, some have it occasionally and some have a lot. Dysphoria can be upsetting, distressing, painful, depressing and isolating. People experience it in different ways. It can be very hard to experience as the dysphoric person and the family/partner. As the dysphoric person, explaining your feelings and what you need from someone else is really helpful and, as the family member or partner, it's important to try to remember that their dysphoria isn't something you can fix – you may get hurt by it sometimes, but just be there for them in whatever ways you can [and] that they are comfortable with." (Shae)

It's important to note that there is no "cure" for gender dysphoria; for some trans people, the solution to ease their dysphoria is to seek out hormones and surgery, but even these are long-term solutions that don't address the distress the person may be feeling in the moment. Some trans people don't see surgery and hormones as a viable solution or may choose to postpone making the decision. This is especially true of non-binary people, who may feel that instead of being misgendered as the gender they were assigned at birth, they will then become misgendered as another gender that still doesn't fit them.

"My partner has been out for a year now, and although he is much more comfortable in himself living as male, he still experiences days where he wants to shut the world out and hide himself away. Having had no surgery, he hates his body; he has been on testosterone since Jan. 2016 and is desperate for the effects to work more quickly. [D]espite his deepening voice and hair growth on his face, it's not enough." (Rene)

It is also worth noting that even after the physical effects of hormones and surgery, some people still experience bouts of dysphoria. While this is normal, you as a partner need to know what to do when your partner is experiencing dysphoria.

Practical tips to help someone experiencing dysphoria

I can't stress enough that you need to keep communicating with your partner about how they want you to help while they are experiencing dysphoria. These tips will not help the dysphoria or make it go away, but they may help your partner cope with the associated feelings.

"My partner's dysphoria was greatest regarding periods and breasts (he had massive DD ones). In terms of how I helped my partner manage that dysphoria, there were few things I could do, apart from supporting him in the decision to transition.

We discussed the feelings, and so I knew more about what not to say than what to say. For example, it was extremely unhelpful for me to say how much I loved his body or that it didn't matter that he had the wrong body." (Sally Rush)

Sit down with your partner and agree on the things on the list below that they would like for you to do. Because it's not an exhaustive list, you may want to add notes about what your own partner wants.

- Talk about it. If your partner wants to talk, it's important to validate what they're going through. Saying things like "I'm so sorry for what you're going through" or "That sounds awful" is a lot more helpful than saying "It's not that bad."

- Don't talk about it. If your partner doesn't want to talk, don't push them. Sometimes, trans people can be frustrated by feeling that they constantly need to explain how they feel.

- Ask how you can help. Sometimes, your partner will have a clear view of what you can do to help, and if they do, try to help in that way.

- Leave them alone; sometimes, your partner will want to spend some time on their own so that they can process what they are going through. If they do need some space, respect their wishes.

- Offer them something that usually makes them feel comforted, like a cup of tea, a blanket and snuggling in for a favourite film.

- Dance! Turn some music on and just dance, even if you don't know how or aren't very good. Just have a silly dance party in the house.

- If you plan in advance, you can create a self-care package which can include herbal tea, sweet treats, perhaps a colouring book and pencils, a good book for them to read, a cuddly toy or anything that you know they will love.

- Go for a walk, run or cycle ride. The physical exertion will get the endorphins going and also keep them healthy.

- Encourage your partner to take up a hobby. This can be building puzzles, making greeting cards, decoupage, sewing, knitting, woodworking, painting, drawing, photography and so on. Just try to make sure that anything you suggest is in line with your partner's interests.

4

Coming Out

This section of the book deals specifically with a partner's coming out journey. Coming out as the partner of a trans person can be complicated, because it is inherently linked to the trans person's coming out.

> "For myself, after all the secrecy which I had to endure while my partner was transitioning, it was a massive relief to be able to finally reconnect with the LGBT community and 'come out' about my relationship, with people who were able to accept both my identity and my relationship as integrated facets of who I was." (Sasha)

Some people don't see coming out as something they need to do, because they aren't changing, only their partner and their situation are. If you never face the hurdle of needing to explain, that's wonderful. For others, though, coming out can be a complicated issue.

> "We were actually really lucky in terms of friends; all our friends accepted her right away. There were some slips in terms of gendering her correctly, but they tried. Her family took a while to come around on name/pronouns but did support her. (Amusingly, her father thought 'HRT' meant she was going to be starting testosterone!) My family, unfortunately, ended up disowning me; my mother had been abusive and manipulative, so this was also the last

straw on my side. To this day, they refuse to recognise that they don't have a son-in-law any more, and transition began almost eight years ago." (Tasha Martin)

The in-between time

Sometimes, the gap between finding out your partner is trans and your ability to talk to someone about it can be very difficult. The most important point to navigate in this in-between time is that your partner being trans is not your story to tell. If your partner has specifically asked you not to tell anyone else, it can be a difficult burden to bear, because the people you may normally rely on for help and advice (for example, friends and family) may be the very people your partner asks you not to tell.

"[My partner] is only out to a few friends and family but can answer this better next year when she will be full time. It may be useful to cover what I call the 'twilight world' which we currently live in which sits between everything until she is full time. This stage can be very difficult and is full of fear of discovery. Two of my children found out by accident (in my blog); however, they have been very supportive. I have told a handful of my own friends, who, again, have been great and very supportive, but none of my partner's friends know. More people know about [my partner] than she thinks, but I think I have subconsciously surrounded myself with friends who I have told and knew they would be accepting, so when she does come out to one and all, there is support for us both. Not one person so far has been negative... [N]ot everyone understands; however, all have been very supportive, including my boss at work. [My partner] is very worried about my family, as we are all very close, and it is this specifically that makes her waver. I think I already know who will be supportive, accepting, accepting but not understanding, and who could possibly cut all ties; however, I know from previously going through a messy divorce, you cannot always predict accurately who will step up to the plate and [who] will shy away. What makes it more difficult is [my partner] has created such a great 'illusion' of being very male/macho that it will make it very difficult for people to understand or even believe the situation." (Avril)

During this time, it is vital that you keep the communication open with your partner, research being trans as much as you can and reach out to online or face-to-face groups for trans partners. You can also consider counselling, either for yourself or as a couple.

Telling the children

Telling children that their parent is trans can be daunting. Your approach will need to be tailored for your children. There is no one-size-fits-all solution.

"As with anything, I've always worked to keep explanations as age appropriate as possible and also to not overwhelm the children with more information than they know what [to] do with. In that vein, the thing I did was provide a basic explanation of what was happening, what it meant [and] how we would act differently (in terms of name or pronoun changes), and then [I] really left it open to questions. I've found that if I share too much, they become bored and distracted because they are overwhelmed with information, but keeping the information simple and answering questions directly has always worked best. More questions will always come up, and it's always going to be an ongoing process. The main thing is to keep the lines of communication open and remind the children that they are free to ask or discuss more in depth when they want to." (Julia)

It's also important to allow the children space to digest the information. They may have questions or need some space to think about what this means. It's crucial to be honest with them and to be there for them while they work through the implications.

> "We are about to tell our 13-year-old daughter at the start of [the upcoming] summer holidays, so [I] can give you an update on this when we have done so. [My partner] shies away from telling her; however, I feel it is necessary for her to know sooner rather than later while [my partner] still looks and acts a bit like her dad (I say a bit, as there have been lots of subtle changes over the past year). I think this is important to give our daughter time to come to terms with the situation and say 'goodbye' to her dad. We also plan on telling her school so they are prepared and can support her. She is friends at school with a trans boy (FTM), which is amazing. We have picked the start of the summer holidays so she has six weeks away from school to assimilate the information and try to make sense of it. I have also taken the first week off, so that we are both around for her, and as [my partner] works nights, she will be there the rest of the time. What seems to be severely lacking is a support group for kids who have a trans parent. GIRES [Gender Identity Research and Education Society] and other organisations [are] more geared toward the child being trans. It would be great if we could point our daughter toward a group of similarly aged children in a similar situation, so there is support if she needs it." (Avril)

You should also be prepared for children not to have a strong reaction when you come out to them. The use of age-appropriate television shows, documentaries and books can help them understand what being trans means.

"My partner was always adamant that there was no way that she would pursue transition if the children were not okay with it. We were fairly confident that the younger two would deal with it, at eight and ten they were young enough to take most things in their stride, but it was the teenagers that were our biggest concern, our eldest the 16-year-old in particular. We decided to tell the older two first, a few days before her first GP appointment to ask for a referral, and we needn't have worried at all. Yes, it was pretty scary, but we talked about her depression which they were already aware of and the fact that we thought we had found the probable cause, then [we] explained that she was transgender. They both took it exceptionally well, with little more than a teenage half shrug and an 'Okay, fair enough.' Neither of them seemed phased in the slightest and have been completely accepting. The eldest told me that as far as he's concerned, if something is affecting your mental health and there's something that you can do about it, you'd be an idiot not to try.

We waited until we'd told most close family before telling the younger two, shortly before her first Gender Identity Clinic [GIC] appointment. We had watched an excellent CBBC programme, *I am Leo*, about a trans boy a few months before, and this meant that they already had some understanding of the concept of being trans, which helped a lot. We talked about daddy having a girl brain but a boy body and that it made her sad and said that we were trying to find a way for her to feel happier. Our youngest responded that it must be very confusing to have a brain like that; he thought that making them match was a good idea. The key thing with all of them has been that we have answered any questions they have willingly and honestly, and also I think knowing early in the process has helped; they felt their views mattered, [and] they had time to process and get their heads around the concept before the rest of the world knew." (Helen)

Children can be hugely supportive as well, and getting them to feel involved with transition can make them feel that they have a part in all this and that their views matter. For many children, it helps to talk about how they will refer to their trans parent to avoid awkward situations when they are out.

> "We were both surprised by the reactions of my four children and the support they gave. The grandchildren took it in their stride, and in some ways they led the way in changing 'she' into 'he' and choosing 'pops' as their name for my partner." (Nicola Kalisky)

Whom to come out to

I separated my coming out from my partner's coming out. If you see it in this way, you find it's probably easier to decide whom to come out to and when. Some people you will come out to as a couple. This is generally people whom your partner will need to come out to, such as your partner's family, common friends and close members of your own family.

> "When my husband came out to his mother, it was a few months after I knew. We had already changed his name socially and pronouns between the both of us and [had] a referral into a GIC, but he felt he was ready for his family to know. He had different reactions from different people. His mother felt he was just a transvestite, his father didn't bring it up for several months, his siblings ignored it for months and his sister refused to tell his niece until he had seen a GIC. When his niece found out by accident before his first appointment, she asked questions and started to not use his birth name and birth pronouns when she was just with us.
>
> My husband made me call his aunt; even though we knew she had a friend who is transgender as well, we were still so nervous about telling her. She is still one of his

biggest supporters, and, like myself, changed his name and pronouns easily." (Anne)

Make a list, if it helps. There are some people whom it is impossible to avoid coming out to. These are likely to be close friends and/or family that you interact with often. These are also the people who may unexpectedly find out anyway.

> "He was so worried about coming out to his family that he wrote a letter and left it for them to open. His mum, dad and sister reacted so positively and spread the word to the rest of the family, who also reacted positively. Everyone can see how much happier he is, and while the older generation occasionally gets the he/him pronouns wrong, none of it is meant maliciously. [I]t's just habit." (Rene)

Separate people that you are friends with from your partner's social group. Also, separate your work friends and colleagues from your partner's work friends and colleagues. There are different implications for trans people's coming out and for that of partners of trans people.

> "Telling people is scary, there's no getting away from that, so we started slowly with the people that we had the most confidence would take it well and be accepting, and [we] built on that. People were divided into two basic groups, people who we felt that we needed to tell personally and everyone else. The first group consisted of close family and friends, and we gradually worked through them, feeling a little braver each time as we received supportive responses. I think perhaps this was helped by the fact that we told most family after her first GIC appointment but before she had firm plans with regards to transition; they then saw some of the journey and weren't shocked by a sudden announcement that everything was changing straight away. Once everyone who needed telling in person

had been told, she had reached a point of wanting to transition, so she posted a message on Facebook explaining everything and [saying] that from now on she would be going by her new name. We've been very lucky in that the response was very supportive and accepting.

On the whole, we've found that people very quickly come to see that she's still the same person she has always been, and whilst some struggle with the name and pronoun change, everyone so far has been willing to try and [is] getting the hang of it." (Helen)

The key to whom to come out to is to consider whether not telling makes you more uncomfortable than telling would. If you aren't close to your colleagues or you just don't talk about family and relationships, then it's not necessary to come out to them. If, however, you are squirming because them using the incorrect pronouns is really bothering you, then tell them.

"My Love is stealth, which means that he doesn't tell new people that he is transgender – very few instances would be exceptions to this. His family all knew before I met him, and some friends/former friends knew. When relevant, he also tells his doctors/nurses. My family don't know, even though he has had stage one (UK) phalloplasty whilst living with us; they just know he has had surgery and aren't interested in asking about it, other than checking he's healing well, etc.

I came out as gender neutral to my mum before I met my boyfriend, and I was open about it on my online profile, so he knew when he first messaged me. I mentioned it to my dad, but he's never really understood it, so he just never talks about it. The rest of my family are all cisgender people in heterosexual relationships, so I don't talk about it with them. My nan knows, but she thinks it's because I was bullied and emotionally abused constantly all through my childhood and have polycystic ovarian syndrome, which means my hormones are wacky.

Some people understand and are supportive. Some people don't understand but are supportive. Some people are neutral and don't talk about it. Some people just refuse to accept it. You can't make anyone do anything, so a loved one being transphobic or just plain unsupportive may hurt, but you have to decide if you can ignore it or if you need to lessen your contact with them for your own health. Whatever may happen, make sure you're safe – it probably isn't the right time to come out if you are at risk, so consider postponing it or having someone to help you stay safe when coming out." (Shae)

Coming out to friends and family

Delivery is also important. If you make it seem like the most normal thing in the world, the people around you have no reason to question whether this is a good thing or not and have less ammunition against you.

"My parents were concerned about my well-being and the strain on our relationship and have had more difficulties in their language and definition of male. My partner had a supportive response from his sibling, but his mother found it difficult. The most amazing response was from his grandmother. She wasn't fazed by the news and acknowledged that she always thought she should have [a] grandson." (Nicola Kalisky)

If your initial reaction to your partner being trans is negative, it's especially important to work through these feelings with someone who isn't invested in your relationship. There are many anecdotes that I've heard where a partner breaks down in front of family or friends, which makes it much harder for them if they later come to accept their partner and continue the relationship through transition. Remember, the people around you will sometimes take their cue for how to react from how you do.

"My partner started living full time while I was working on a project. I didn't really know how to tell people; I didn't feel comfortable telling everyone at once or sending a mass email out. So, I decided to take a pragmatic route and tell people as it came up in conversation. I would refrain from any mention of my partner, and if anyone asked about him, I would correct them and tell them that my partner is now a woman. If they wanted to know more, I would inform them, but I didn't make it my mission to spread the word about trans issues or be a trans activist. I thought, just for now, for me, I have to make this a little thing. Not an all-encompassing big thing.

The first person I told was my manager. This allowed me a safety net just in case I had to face something nasty. It was surprisingly easy after that. I found that the environment I was in allowed me to only explain to a few key people, because most people didn't ask." (Jo)

People take their cues from you. If you are visibly upset about it, people will show concern for you and not see transition as a positive thing. This doesn't mean that you aren't allowed to show any emotion, but choose it carefully. Explain to people that you realise that this is the best thing for your partner but it is complicated, and explain the things you are scared of losing but also explain what you may be gaining.

"In terms of the reactions of others, they weren't as bad as expected. [W]hen he did get hassle, we learnt how to handle it, as I say, primarily by identifying the safe toilets. We learnt to stop living in fear and to enjoy each day much more.

His parents did struggle, and that was an interesting one. I listened and made sure I used the right pronouns as I affirmed I understood some of the things they were saying about how they felt.

One strategy I found really useful was to ensure we went out to eat when he had had a medical appointment.

It was easier to talk about it over dinner, because it was less likely to end up in an argument or misunderstanding. I guess in a public setting you just ask the questions you need to know, like 'how long?', 'what next?' and so on. You both have to keep your emotions under control as you discuss scary things." (Sally Rush)

Be warned, though, some people will be massively curious and want to know intimate details (I once got asked by a colleague how we have sex, which I wouldn't dream of answering in any other situation, so I politely refused to answer).

As time passes, you'll need to come out less and less. I used simple tricks; for example, I referred to my partner as my partner and avoided any mention of gender as far as possible. If someone else used the wrong pronoun, I would correct them, but I tried not to mention my personal life. If worst comes to worst, change the subject and swiftly move on. There's no need to put yourself in an uncomfortable or compromising position if you don't want to.

The coming out discussion

If you are helping your partner come out to your friends and family, it's a good idea to have a face-to-face discussion. There are some tips in the following sections about things I took into consideration, but these won't apply to everyone, so disregard them if they make you feel uncomfortable or you don't agree.

Don't have the meeting in a public place. If it does turn very sour, you don't want to be in a position where you could be humiliated in public. Having it at your home is also not a good idea. Try having it at the person's house; this gives you an opportunity to leave should you feel uncomfortable.

Have the meeting separately; don't come out to a huge group. This will allow you to get the person's unbiased reaction, away from the people that may influence them.

The important thing to remember about coming out as a couple is that you need to come out as a team. You need to be in it together. You should put aside reservations that you personally may have and face this together. The reactions you get will not always be supportive, and you need to prepare for this. However, not everything is doom and gloom; these are the worst-case scenarios. I found that coming out was a lot easier than I thought. I had dreaded it and felt like everyone was going to hate me and think I was a freak, but what actually happened was that people were generally supportive and even those who weren't that supportive didn't run screaming.

"We were anxious about telling various people, and it's probably easier to describe the main ones...

Her parents – mum knew since she was 15 that she had these feelings but told her to ignore them. Dad was surprisingly okay. Both now pretend to be okay, but they still refer to her in her old name and with masculine pronouns accidentally.

Her brother – refused to invite her to his wedding. They now don't talk.

My parents – my dad was very angry, as he felt we had hidden it from him and he was the last to know. Now he seems okay with it all, although he regularly asks me to talk to her about how she dresses (apparently, it is not appropriate for a 32-year-old to wear short skirts). Not sure how my stepmum feels – she doesn't really say much about it.

Friends – this has been varied. Everyone has been great to our face, but we have later found out that some friends have been using it as gossip behind our backs (telling other people and laughing about it). As a result, we have lost over half of our friendship group, but the friends we have now are much stronger and closer relationships." (Stevie)

Coming out at work

Coming out at work can feel really scary, but it doesn't need to be done all at once. A big company announcement usually isn't necessary, but I have a few tips that may help.

> "I was scared to death that she'd lose her job, and I begged her to hold off on telling them for as long as she could. She did try, but the effects of HRT outed her after a couple of months. After all that panic, though, her employer was very supportive; they changed her name long before it was done legally/officially, and they backed her against occasional instances of transphobia at work. (She was immediately allowed to use the right bathroom, too; that shouldn't be an issue, but it is.) She has since left that job simply because it was time to move on in her career, and her new employer has treated transition as a non-issue, since it happened long before she arrived." (Tasha Martin)

If you work in the same company, the contrast in support for trans people versus the support for partners can be very obvious.

> "It became increasingly difficult for Davina on a Monday morning to put her few remaining male clothes on. [M]ost people knew her as Davina, [and] she looked so unhappy and dejected; I nagged her to come out at work, and together we agreed [on] a date.
>
> Davina went to HR at The Company. The Company has a process, which was duly followed. [B]ecause her son worked at The Company, they had a duty of care to go speak to him, as he refused prior to her coming out as Davina to communicate with his dad. There was no communication to where I worked in The Company, even though I was working with a group of Davina's colleagues. I told the people I worked with, because I was finding it increasingly difficult to swap names and pronouns. ... The

fact we worked in the same company, for many years in the same department, [meant that] people knew both of us. The fact that my husband was standing up and declaring to the world she was a woman was nothing to do with me... The Company supported her, and it had nothing to do with me, [and] they did not owe me a duty of care. I struggled with this attitude and felt it did affect me; no thought was given to how people reacted to me.

I took Davina out and helped her buy a wardrobe of clothes for work and she looked stunning. Everyone was lovely to her.

I had a few emails and phone calls as the news got out; it was hot gossip and it spread like wildfire. I did have emails; people wanted to know if I was aware before we married, if we were still together, etc. [A] few people apologised, [and] some laughed at me, [saying] does that make you a lesbian... Not nice, but hey, it was nothing to do with me. Davina was happy and accepted." (Linda)

Tell human resources (HR)

First off, speak to your HR representative. They may be able to guide you as to the company policy. Discussions with your HR representative should also be confidential (but make sure of that). This is just to forewarn them should there be any negative impacts when you start telling your management and colleagues.

I cannot stress enough that you need to be prepared. Take some information with you, look online for leaflets or information regarding trans issues, and perhaps research the company policy on workplace discrimination.

Tell your manager

The next person to speak to will be your direct supervisor or manager. This is for a number of reasons:

- Forewarning – telling your manager or supervisor first will allow them to be prepared should there be any negative repercussions from your colleagues.

- Time off – you may want to advise your manager that you may need to take some days off at strange times to go with your partner to doctor appointments, specialist consultations, etc. If you are having a difficult time, you may need to take some time to get away from it all. Also, inform them of the timeline for your partner's surgery (if that applies to you), so that they know to expect you to take some time off around then to assist your partner.

- Company events – explaining that your partner is trans and may not be comfortable coming to company functions, such as Christmas parties, office picnics and so on, will save you from having to make excuses about why they won't be attending. This also applies if your partner does want to attend events; the management team is aware of it and can make sure that you are not put in an awkward position.

"What I did do as soon as I knew the time scale they were giving for surgery, which was helpful, was let my work know that he was having an operation and I would need to amend my desk time slightly to help care for him [and] get this agreed [on] in writing. I didn't go into details, but it meant that I had that confidence it had been agreed in advance." (Sally Rush)

Telling colleagues

This can sometimes be tricky. With your close colleagues, I suggest that you tell one person at a time when it comes up in conversation; for example, if someone asks after your partner, tell them that your partner is trans and is now living full time as the other gender (if this is appropriate). When I came out at work, I was surprised at how easy it was. By sticking to my rule of only telling anyone who asked after my partner, I found that after the close colleagues (whom I counted as friends), it didn't really come up in conversation.

Coming out: questions and responses

Make sure that you are ready for the questions. There will be questions aimed at both of you, and some will be aimed at you specifically.

> "We went to see our favourite wedding singer at a venue; her mother was there and asked questions, like how did we have sex now... [I] found it strange, but soon realised many of our friends, when Davina was not there, would ask me questions about her transition. I answered honestly [with] all I knew; stupid as it sounds, she was Davina, took hormones and wanted to be acknowledged and known as a woman.
>
> I lost count of the number of times I was asked if I was now a lesbian. I always answered [that] I am not a lesbian and because of my health we do not have a sex life." (Linda)

I've listed some of the questions with my suggestions below:

"What do you think of all this?"

Be supportive if you are asked this question directly. This is not the time or the place to bring out all the issues you and your partner may be having. If you aren't completely okay with it, be vague. You can say something along the lines of you are still surprised but you are very supportive, you love each other very much, and you are willing to work together on trying to figure out what this means for your marriage/relationship.

"Oh, so does that mean he will want to marry a man?"

This is a question often asked of the partners of trans women. It seems that in a heteronormative society, people assume that trans women will leave to be with a man (I've not yet heard of this being asked about trans men or non-binary people). Remind them that sexuality and gender are different things. Your partner identifies as a different gender; that doesn't automatically mean that they are changing sexuality. It can also be a good opportunity to correct their use of the wrong pronoun and explain what misgendering is.

"Has he/she always known?"

Try to direct the question back to your partner, if they are there. This isn't for you to answer on your partner's behalf. If you're on your own, it can be an opportunity to talk about being trans and what it means (and dispelling the narrative of always having known). You can also feel free to say that you are not comfortable speaking on your partner's behalf.

Expect the personal questions that you may not want to answer and have a response ready for these, too, even if it is just saying that you don't really feel comfortable speaking about it.

The uncomfortable questions

The following questions are ones that many partners are asked. All these are insensitive, and you are under no obligation to answer.

- When is your partner having the surgery?

- What does he/she look like?

- How do you have sex?

- Did you know from the beginning?

- Are you embarrassed to go out in public?

- Do they wear a wig?

- Do they have boobs?

The unsupportive support

One of the key things that I faced when I came out to my friends and family was the unsupportive support. This is when friends and family really don't support being or staying in a relationship with a trans person because they are transphobic (even if it is just mildly transphobic). These people will be the ones who are more than happy to be around and offer support when things are not going well, but they are not willing to share in the joys. They can often be identified as the ones who, when they see you, ask patronisingly, "How are you doing?" (often accompanied by a slight head tilt). These are generally people who do not have your best interests at heart. They honestly believe that you will be better off leaving the relationship and finding someone who isn't trans.

These can be the most dangerous people to a relationship which is already unsteady from having to deal with trans issues, because their influence can make you believe that you are a victim of the situation. The way to deal with these people is not to cut contact with them (because they are often close friends and family) but rather to only show them the good parts. You will be able to get support from other friends, other partners of trans people (seek them out, because they do exist) and mental health professionals. Do not rely on the destructive people in your life.

"The hardest thing was coming out to our lesbian community. I received an email from someone on a lesbian group I was involved with, saying 'now you're straight; you shouldn't be on here' – the ignorance was astonishing. We lost a lot of our sense of community, and there was a process of mourning – I'm pleased to say that three years on, we feel part of a much more inclusive, open community, but it was tough for a bit. We found out who our friends were, and they really stuck by us. Funnily enough, our straight world was much easier – straight friends, family and work accepted the change much more readily." (Ricky)

5

Sexuality

One of the biggest challenges that many partners face is in terms of their sexuality, either because their view of their own sexuality changes or because even if it doesn't, other people's view of it may still do.

"Our relationship has been based on negotiation through the transition and working together to ensure that the essential parts of our relationship, which are based on far more than primary or secondary sex characteristics, are not lost. If we adopt the word queer and say we are in a queer relationship it reflects the reality of what is going on, particularly as my husband is a man but one who is aware of the risks of genital reconstruction and so is not taking that route through transition.

The world may see it as straight, and that is fine (it is far easier than when my partner gets misgendered because they see two people of a similar height together). However, we know there is more than that going on. Embracing the word queer allows the whole situation to be embraced.

You might wonder why it has taken me so much time to get here...well, in part, because somebody wise at the beginning of the journey said it was the loss of identity and issues around that which were most likely to see us not make it through. Thus it is an area I have sought at times to avoid really thinking about.

Having sat and thought it through, though, I think it helps that I find intellectual attraction stronger than physical attraction, and so the physical change has not been so difficult for me. [T]he decisions regarding which surgery to have and not have [that] my partner has made for safety reasons have also helped." (Sally Rush)

Someone once told me that she thought it's harder for people who identify as gay or lesbian before their partner transitions, because being gay or lesbian is an identity that they have spent a lot of time thinking about, working on and often fighting for. Being gay or lesbian created a sense of community with people who identify the same way, and losing that identity is very difficult when they become read as straight as their partner transitions.

Often, they will face questions of whether they were ever "really" gay or lesbian or they were actually straight all along. There are also sometimes issues where they cannot go as a couple to the same social activities (such as pubs and nightclubs), because they get read as straight and aren't allowed in unless they provide a detailed explanation.

"I came out at 16 as a lesbian. When my husband and I first met we were 17 and 19. He was my first 'girlfriend' and is still my first and only relationship. Since he came out as FTM transgender, I have been going over and over how I can describe my predominately same-sex attractions while I have a male husband. I have since not really decided what to say if I am asked, although it is no one's business, but right now I use queer. I don't mind being perceived as straight, as there is nothing wrong with being heterosexual, just like there is nothing wrong with being homosexual." (Anne)

For straight people, the issue can be reversed and can be deeply rooted in straight privilege. They have always been straight, and now they are being viewed by the outside world as being lesbian or gay.

"I find being called a lesbian really difficult, as that is not how I identify myself." (Stevie)

Straight people have also not necessarily gone through the process of understanding different sexualities, outside of what they are going through with their partner. For these people, doing the same social activities can be equally complicated if they've only ever been used to primarily straight spaces.

"As for the sexuality bit, it's a huge question, but one that as yet just doesn't feel like a big deal for me. Yes, I've always identified as straight, but none of the relationships I've ever had have started with physical attraction. I've always got to know someone, fallen for their personality, and then attraction has followed. I'm the same with people in films; I have to like the character before I consider someone attractive! I've come to feel that the term pansexual fits me best; I'm attracted to the person, not the package, [and] it just so happens that before now I only ever fell for guys! Will people perceive me as a lesbian? Possibly, although we've never been particularly publicly affectionate kind of people, so holding hands in public isn't really something we'd do much anyway. Does it worry me if they do? Not really; it would be odd, but I'm not one to worry much about what the world thinks of me. I'm taking this one step at a time and will work it out as I go. [A]s I said, pansexual seems to fit me best right now, but I'm learning more about myself all the time, so who knows? I've been asking myself all sorts of questions that I never considered in my youth!" (Helen)

That being said, maintaining the status quo with your sexual and social identity can become very difficult for a couple. There is inherently the question of whether an unchanging orientation implies that on some level you don't see your partner's gender as what they say it is or that the relationship is doomed to fail (because at some point you are going to inevitably want to be with a partner who more closely matches your sexuality).

> "Personally, I don't think someone's sexuality needs to change because their partner's gender identity has, unless they want it to – though some guys can feel uncomfortable with their partner identifying as a lesbian whilst they identify as a man. Some people realise they are pansexual or bisexual because their partner is transitioning. Others still identify as lesbians, as they'd only be dating women if they weren't already in love with their partner, or they'd go back to only being with women if their current relationship didn't work out, etc.
>
> I've always been heteromantic, and I've only ever seen my boyfriend as a regular guy; it's never been about him being cis or trans, so I don't feel like I'm panromantic just because he is transgender. He's also heteromantic and doesn't see himself as panromantic just because I'm gender neutral."
> (Shae)

While labels are important to us, it's important to realise that a label is no longer useful if it is doing more harm than good. If your relationship with your partner should end, I firmly believe it should be for bigger reasons than just the label you use. This obviously doesn't mean that I'm advocating you change your identity to suit your partner, but with some flexibility, you can find labels that you feel more comfortable with and that better explain your sexuality.

> "I'm still trying to get my head around this. The identifications of sexuality are new to me. I don't go out on the scene, so I haven't had to come out. My friends still identify me as lesbian, but it's still early days, and my partner hasn't undergone surgery as yet." (Nicola Kalisky)

Many of these issues aren't faced by people who identify as bisexual (people who are attracted to both people of their own gender as well as other genders) or pansexual (sexually attracted to people irrespective of gender).

> "I was fortunate in that I was bisexual and preferred women even before my partner was one. I have definitely found it challenging at times to navigate the world as a perceived lesbian, and we both miss aspects of straight privilege (nobody used to assume we were sisters or ask where our husbands were during our anniversary dinner!). However, I have never approached it as 'coming out' so much as revealing details of my life; I flinch a little internally every time I say 'my wife' for the first time, but I act as if it's a perfectly normal part of small talk. So far, no one has ever reacted badly, either.
>
> The other frustrating thing is that I was presumed to be straight before, and I'm presumed to be a lesbian now. My sexuality is not and has never been defined by my partner's gender, but that's the default assumption. Being taken for a lesbian is less wrong, but it's still wrong, and no matter how many times I mention that I'm bisexual, people tend to forget that fact again." (Tasha Martin)

As the makeup of relationships change, there is also a new language developing to encompass some of these changes; some examples are as follows:

- hetero-flexible: primarily heterosexual, but flexible

- homo-flexible: primarily homosexual, but flexible

- demisexual: part of the asexual spectrum, only sexually attracted to someone if there is an emotional connection (irrespective of gender)

- androsexual: sexually attracted to masculinity (irrespective of gender)

- femmesexual/gynosexual: sexually attracted to femininity (irrespective of gender)

- queer: generic term for people who identify as not straight. There is some discussion that people who are in a "straight" relationship with a trans person are queer by default.

- skoliosexual: sexually attracted to people who are non-binary, genderqueer or outside of binary genders

- omnisexual: sexually attracted to someone irrespective of gender.

"I identify as a woman for work (in that way, I suppose I'm in stealth), and I suppose that also allows me to express the side of me that represents the gender I was assigned at birth. However, when I'm not at work, I'm more fluid; depending on the day, I can either represent as firmly non-binary or as slightly more feminine. I don't ever really identify as male, which is where I found the label of demifeminine useful. I'm sort of somewhere between non-binary and female.

I also think that this is hugely influenced by my identity as a feminist. I don't think that I'll ever fully be able to give up being a woman, because my experiences being raised as a girl have fundamentally shaped how I see myself and the relationship I have to my body. But I don't really see myself as fully in the woman camp either.

As a side note, I identify as a dyke but not as a lesbian. To me, it feels like lesbian is firmly for binary women who like binary women. Dyke feels like it has more wiggle room in the definition." (Jo)

And if none of these labels fit your situation, create a new one. Labels should be there to help us define ourselves; they should not be there to restrict us.

"Sometimes, it is easiest to let go of the labels and let people simply be people." (Sally Rush)

Some people feel really strongly that their partner has nothing to do with their sexual identity, and needing to discuss and change it can be very traumatic.

"I didn't feel as though my sexuality had changed. Prior to my relationship with my trans partner, I had had relationships with both men and women, and was happy defining as lesbian, but I had kind of given up looking for a 'label' which people would understand. During our relationship, I discovered the term pansexual, and felt that the description I found on Wikipedia summed up how I felt about my sexual orientation. Now that I am no longer in the relationship, I have found myself less likely to keep using pansexual to describe myself and more likely to use lesbian. It seems to be influenced by who my friends are and who is in my social circle." (Sasha)

Others feel that perhaps having a defined sexuality isn't that important at all.

"I've never really thought of myself as having any definitive sexuality. I fall for the person, not the package they come in. I don't know what causes transgenderism, and I find it a fascinating subject, but also one that must be very frustrating for trans people. Not enough research has been done to find out more about transgenderism, but at least more is being done to educate the world about it.

I joke that I was a lesbian for five minutes, and now I'm straight again. I've never really pinned my sexuality down or labelled myself in any way, so I don't see myself as changing sexuality anyway." (Rene)

6

A Partner's Gender Identity

It's becoming increasingly common for partners to also re-evaluate their gender identity while their partner transitions as well as for partners who are themselves trans to be in a relationship with a trans person.

"I was already very involved with trans people and the trans community myself, although not out as trans (nonbinary was still an emerging identity at the time). I knew that my partner had a male gender identity, and I knew my own gender identity was complicated. I felt that us being lesbians and being part of a community where gender is played with a lot kind of worked, even though it rested on the idea of seeing yourself primarily as a woman and exclusively orientated to other women. We were both bisexual but kept that to ourselves. The community was almost a good fit, but some parts of us were being stifled. When my partner came out as a trans man, it shook things up for me. At first I was upset, and I quickly realised I was upset because of what his coming out was going to mean for my own declared identity. Despite describing myself as a lesbian, the real issue for me was my gender identity, not my sexuality. So yes, his transition got me thinking a bit more deeply about identity, and also about the foolishness of us defining who we are based on who our partner is, or worse, some superficial label they were given at birth." (Ricky)

Realising that gender isn't fixed and that you have a choice in how you identify and how you present can be hugely empowering for partners.

"Before I knew anything about trans things, I was blissfully operating in a world where I could sometimes conform to gender stereotypes and sometimes not. I lived in a weird utopia where I didn't need to define my gender or my identity. If I did girl things, that was expected; if I did boy things, I was being a tomboy or a feminist. If women were limited to only performing certain things, that was the fault of the patriarchy; if they went ahead anyway, it was taken that they were strong and brave.

And then I fell in love with a trans woman. I was so ridiculously cis that trans wasn't even something I'd heard of. I understood her feelings of worthlessness, [and] I empathised with her feeling of always being the other, of never feeling worthy of love. I empathised so much that I drew her into my arms and wouldn't let her go. She was the mirror image of me; she was the missing piece of my soul. I would do anything to help her feel better, feel loved, feel worthy.

So I started reading. I read anything that was published about trans experiences, I was well versed in the treatment pathways and the Harry Benjamin Standards of Care. I turned her journey into something I could fix. I would help her, and by helping, I would fix the part of me that was broken, too.

But that's just it; by helping her, I started realising that there were cracks in my idea of who I am. In the face of someone who was fighting so hard to be seen as a woman, I realised that I had nothing invested in my label of woman. I was massively invested in the label of strong, but not the label of woman. When faced with the narratives of 'I've always felt like a woman', I had no words. I'd never felt like a woman; I didn't know what that meant.

I now identify as non-binary. I am figuring out my own treatment pathways, because the medical profession only knows how to treat binary trans people (and it's already bursting at the seams just trying to manage that). I can honestly say that if it wasn't for my wife being trans and us getting involved in the trans community, I think it may never have occurred to me that I can actually get treatment and feel better about myself." (Jo)

This intersection of gender identity and sexuality can become complex as well, because how you are perceived within the queer community may change as you, your partner or both of you transition.

"My partner and I are both bisexual. We identified as lesbians publicly and were a big part of the lesbian community. I think the biggest shock in transition has been the change in how people see us – me being seen as a straight woman when I'm a non-binary bisexual person. But people look at you and look at your partner and put you in a box. Neither of our sexualit[ies] has changed, but perceptions have. The good thing has been being more out about being bisexual and realising the bisexual community is less uptight about labels. Neither of us had really faced before how we lived as lesbians and called ourselves [that] when we knew we were bisexual." (Ricky)

Finding help when you exist at the intersection of gender and sexuality can be even more complicated, because counsellors will sometimes assume that your issues are all about one specific aspect (usually gender identity). It's also true that sometimes the bad experiences from one partner may provide an element of what to expect for the other.

"I haven't gone through gender therapy yet (on the waiting list), and I don't know much about My Love's experiences with it or any therapy – other than the fact that one mental health help attempt at university was met with the person insisting his depression was solely because he is transgender and didn't listen to him that only some of it was, so it didn't help him.

I've had multiple attempts at counselling, and I gave up for a little while because, whilst I never brought up my gender identity back then, they were never understanding and always manipulated what I said, dismissing lots of it. I gave up with therapy for a while, because I lost trust in ever finding one that would listen to me. Now I'm waiting for one that helps people with chronic pain/illnesses deal with how it affects their mental health. I'm on the waiting list for gender therapy, and I'm also waiting to get one-on-one general mental health counselling." (Shae)

7

Sex

Because of a trans person's dysphoria, sex can sometimes be very difficult to discuss; this becomes especially complicated as a trans person transitions and their role changes. Add to this the changes in a partner's sexuality, and you have the start of a very volatile situation, if you don't address it.

> "When my partner started on the T, he became highly sexualised, which I didn't really mind. I wasn't bothered about him watching porn or thinking about sex a lot. However, his ability to connect with me as a person during sex ceased, and I quickly started to feel unsafe during sex with him. He seemed to get clumsier and would make really inappropriate judgments, like, for instance, ripping all his clothes off when I was nowhere near ready for that moment! He didn't seem to have any idea how it would make me feel. It really put me on edge. He wouldn't talk to me about it, so things just deteriorated from there. Prior to the T, we had a very good, trusting sexual relationship.
>
> Mainly, it was the change to his sexuality [and] the extreme decreased ability to communicate which were the problems. Although we did later find out that he was also dyspraxic." (Sasha)

It's vital to keep the discussion open and understand that you will need to talk about your individual needs and your needs as a couple.

"Due to my disability, I am in pain, which makes sexual contact difficult anyhow. It is difficult for my partner, whose sex drive has increased, whilst pain is a problem for me due to my disability presently." (Nicola Kalisky)

I would suggest that you start talking about sex in the relationship as early as possible, because keeping the dialogue open can help you if things get complicated later on.

"Our sex life changed the moment I knew my partner was trans. Apart from the obvious added appendage that she currently has, we very much treat each other like two females. I thought that she would not want to use what she has, but her take on it is that this is what she has at the moment and it feels good, so [she] will use it while she has it, even though when dressing she does whinge about the extra 'junk' she has and cannot wait to be rid of it." (Avril)

Your history as sexual partners can also impact how you approach sex together as a couple.

"It helped a great deal that we had been together for a long time (we were each other's first partner). It was still good to talk through what she needed or wanted from time to time, but I was fairly good at noticing the signals that she was uncomfortable. I also switched fairly early to mentally seeing her as a woman, which she said she could pick up on and that it helped. In general, our sex life shifted to being more 'lesbian', meaning that we focused on activities that could be done without/while ignoring a penis. I actually preferred this, so this was one aspect that didn't distress me at all; I had nearly always found 'penetrative' sex uncomfortable to painful at first." (Tasha Martin)

It's worth noting that hormones can have an impact on sex drive and different aspects of sex. Testosterone blockers (for people with testes) can dramatically drop a person's sex drive (although estradiol can also have an impact), but this won't mean that they don't want to have sex; it may just mean that they are less likely to initiate it.

> "The start of hormones has resulted in the decline of penetrative sex – we now don't/can't have any. We have experimented with toys, but it didn't quite seem like my kind of thing. We now have an intimate relationship with a very tentative sex life – my wife's sex drive is now very low (as a result of the hormones), so she doesn't want me to touch her very much. She is happy to perform oral sex or use her fingers on me, but it feels very one-sided. Hopefully this will change once the hormone levels have settled down or after surgery, although I now have worries about 'pleasuring' a woman." (Stevie)

On the other hand, taking testosterone can increase a person's sex drive and it may be that you need to negotiate the timing and frequency of sex. You'll need to talk to your partner about it, because it's only by creating a comfortable safe space that you will be able to open up about what both your needs are and work out solutions if these aren't being met.

> "We were also warned about his sex drive increasing [and] that some people even split because it is too much for the partner to take. I honestly didn't expect that to be an issue; I always had a high sex drive and felt that if he was to match me, that would be okay. I was wrong; mine has slowly gone down, while his is still so high that I feel guilty for not wanting sex much at all.
>
> He is also on a hormone blocker, and while the body heat that comes from that is great in winter, it causes me to feel like I have hot flushes in summer." (Anne)

However, transition can be a time to really get creative with your sex life. It'll take the pressure off the both of you if you're both getting involved in something completely new.

> "As with any couple, we have our peaks and troughs in the bedroom. We have very open communications about likes and dislikes and are both open to trying new things. My partner's appetite was insatiable when he first started testosterone, and I was worried that I wouldn't keep up. But we keep talking, and we try to keep things exciting." (Rene)

Not communicating can create a barrier between you, especially if you don't talk about the details of exactly how you approach sex once your partner has come out.

> "For a few months, I avoided sex with my husband after he came out. I didn't know how to address his sexual body parts. He eventually pulled me up on it, [and] we had an honest discussion about what my problem was and what we did and didn't want to do. We have learnt to communicate about what is comfortable for both of us. I stopped using 'female' words to describe his lower region and switched over to 'male' words, which helped us both in sex. We also looked into and eventually bought sex toys that imitate a phallus to see if that was something he would like to have and if I would enjoy that during our intimate moments.
>
> Knowing he is getting closer and closer to having surgery to remove the 'feminine' aspects of his body, I feel like I need to enjoy them while they are here because I still like them; but [I] try to not focus on them at the same time, as I know his body will become more masculine over time and those 'feminine' parts will no longer be a part of him." (Anne)

Start slowly, and talk openly and often about what you are interested in, what you'd like to try and what works for you and what doesn't. What works for you may also change if your partner gets different types of surgery and their relationship with their body changes.

"For the first few months, we were quite free together, with my extreme self-consciousness being more prominent than his dysphoria. We were each other's firsts and the closeness was incredible. However, that freedom became more restricted as his lower dysphoria started surfacing. It went from frequent to random and often disconnected. His libido, even on testosterone, is almost non-existent.

Until we met and fell for each other, we were asexual (don't experience sexual attraction); we didn't know whether we'd want sexual things or not. However, being intimate and then having it limited by his dysphoria raised an issue of different libidos and different needs for affection. I'm a very affectionate person, and intimacy helps me with my severe body image issues, whereas his dysphoria and very low libido mean intimacy is difficult for him. It's something we're going to have to work on to find a compromise/middle ground. Hopefully the phalloplasty will help ease his dysphoria, and he will eventually be free of it – for us as a couple, but mostly for his quality of life." (Shae)

If your partner goes through surgery, the sexual experience will change, and it's important to talk about how you are going to approach sex as part of the recovery process. When you do resume having sex, take it slowly. Take time to re-explore each other's bodies and work out what works best for both of you.

"My husband has not chosen to have phalloplasty, and so sex has not changed too much. There have been some key points of change though after surgery. Before his top surgery, my husband was really worried about how it would be with his scars, but we just found different foreplay became important. As I write, he has just had his hysterectomy, and so we are going through a six-week period of abstinence. He is worried about it being really different afterwards, but I don't think it will be too different. We'll see." (Sally Rush)

8

Mental Health, Counselling and Therapy

Trans people are more likely than the cis population to have mental health issues, which are caused by a long history of gender dysphoria and/or chronic minority stress rather than by being trans (World Professional Association for Transgender Health, 2011). Minority stress is the increased stress of being part of a minority group, and it is due to the lack of awareness in the general population and consequent discrimination faced by people in a minority.

> "I think the worst of this aspect was when my partner was growing up and the times when she contemplated suicide. This was at a time when there was no internet or groups visibly available. I feel very fortunate that my partner confided in me very early in our relationship, and the past 15 years, it has been a journey we have made together. I do have to reassure her that [I] will always be there for her, which I will be, and have given it lots of thought to be sure that this is a situation I can cope with and am happy to be in." (Avril)

According to the World Professional Association for Transgender Health (WPATH), trans people can present with a number of mental health concerns, such as depression, anxiety and self-harm. They also present with compulsivity, substance abuse or sexual concerns, as well as being more likely to have suffered a history of abuse or neglect. Trans people are also more likely to suffer personality disorders, eating disorders or psychotic disorders. WPATH also notes that trans people are more likely to present with autistic spectrum disorders.

> "I have learned to work with my partner's mental health needs. [I] have learned cues that help me know when he is feeling anxious or stressed, and [I] encourage him to talk if he needs to or to seek medical assistance if there's a need for that kind of support. It's definitely *not* something to be ignored or avoided, and in most cases, it's a requirement for the transition process." (Julia)

These mental health concerns should not, however, impact a person's ability to receive support and treatment. It just means that any treatment plan also must take their mental health needs into consideration. This actually facilitates the treatment for gender dysphoria, as it can assist people in providing informed consent in the transition process (World Professional Association for Transgender Health, 2011).

> "I think he already had depression before completely realising he was transgender, as a result of his childhood, but his dysphoria and experiences as a trans person have made it much worse.
>
> When he's feeling dysphoric, he often shuts me out, and he is someone who requires a lot of space sometimes, even though he also feels lonely. His depression is unpredictable, and he isn't used to expressing himself, so he struggles to explain how he feels and can say things he later says he didn't mean. His feelings about general things can change too, depending on his mood and how much being trans is affecting him at the time – e.g. a good memory can sometimes be remembered sourly because he wasn't fully transitioned at the time.

As for me, I have post-traumatic stress disorder, anxiety, depression and severe body image issues that have kept me almost completely isolated for years. Being transgender hasn't really affected or been affected by them, other than the dysphoria I get. I always get dysphoric during my cycle, and it can last for weeks, so my dysphoria can last that long too. I feel very low and usually want lots of affection to comfort me — it can be difficult for my boyfriend to do that sometimes, which results in me not feeling comfortable being touched at all, because my body-related depression is then added on top of my dysphoria depression.

When mental illnesses are involved, communication and honesty are really important — it's not always easy (ours is a work in progress), but a lot of things can be misunderstood or just left unknown, which can make things worse." (Shae)

This being said, it is also important to factor your own mental health needs into the equation. You need to be able to look after yourself before you try to look after someone else. Transition can be very stressful at times, and these stressors can exacerbate existing mental health concerns.

"I've always had some issues with anxiety and mildly obsessive thinking, and I don't deal well with change. Transition was a tremendous amount of change and unpredictability in a very short period (my wife went from realising she might be trans to finished with transition in 11 months). Unfortunately, that triggered a full-blown anxiety disorder that I am still struggling with. I don't think it was her fault by any means; my personal wiring meant that I was predisposed toward this result. However, there were definitely times when my obsessive anxiety and her dysphoria and depression combined to form a truly awful spiral. She is now on antidepressants, I rely on anti-anxiety meds when necessary, and we've both worked hard on developing better coping skills, but neither of us is ever going to be 'cured'." (Tasha Martin)

The ability to communicate openly about issues beyond transition can ease a lot of the stress of going through transition.

"I suffer with depression/anxiety, and my partner has BPD [borderline personality disorder]. Now that everything is out in the open about both of our ailments and he is living as he has always wanted to, we are both a lot more stable within ourselves and therefore able to support each other if necessary." (Rene)

Nevertheless, not all of a person's mental health issues are about being trans, and the assumption that all their issues are gender related can prevent people from accessing treatment.

"The mental health of my partner generally improved after coming out as trans and particularly when he had started transitioning. He had gone to counselling about other stuff going on in the run-up to coming out as trans and had some prior [visits] to the GP re the trans stuff. That meant he was able to distinguish what was trans related and what came from other stuff. As he began to transition and there were initial issues of misgendering, he did get down, but as I say, it has seen his overall mental health improve so much because he was transitioning.

My own mental health has also improved. Partly because I got to the stage where it was not good, and my GP decided that it must be because of the transition and then being able to find out, no, it wasn't. My counsellor and I worked out that the problem was work and nothing to do with the transition. My counsellor was able to affirm how well I had handled my partner's transition. I think this shows it is important not to put everything down to the transition and trust your own instincts about what is going on rather

than being dragged into others' misunderstandings."
(Sally Rush)

However, even if you are the most supportive partner, transition is stressful. The long waiting lists to see gender specialists, the time it takes between appointments, the legal transition and the need to jump through hoops to be able to meet the criteria for hormones and surgery can take their toll. Being part of a strong support network, especially one that's in the trans community, can be a massive help.

"Don't underestimate the stress of transition. Although ultimately I think we both feel stronger now, there has been a huge upheaval in our lives – changing community, changing identity, the demands of medical appointments and everyday transphobia really take their toll. Support for both of you is really important – things you can access together and separately. I think I was lucky being non-binary, because I had access to support from the community myself and could share some spaces, but it was important my partner had his own spaces too, just for him – particularly around medical changes he wanted that I didn't. I can't recommend enough getting involved with the local trans community and networking, but you have to be willing to see past differences and diverse ways of seeing things and also be really aware of internalised transphobia when you interact with other trans people. They are the experts, but we are so often taught to look down on them, and we don't always notice we're doing it." (Ricky)

It can also be very difficult for partners of trans people to access counselling and therapy. Many of the gender clinics are set up specifically to deal with trans people and offer no support for partners and families. If you do get counselling, you may find that your counsellor doesn't actually understand how to deal with the specific issues a partner has.

"I was in therapy while I was with my partner, but I didn't consider that my therapist understood my relationship at all, as he was a heterosexual man! When I wrote my newsletter about being a partner, he read it, and made a point of apologising to me because, as he said it, he had not understood what I was going through." (Sasha)

It's important to find the right therapist, so you may need to try several to find the one that works for you.

"I have been fortunate enough to find a couple of counsellors who have dealt with trans couples and/or partners of BPD sufferers, and that has helped enormously with my own state of mind. I have also attended a meditation course, which has been useful in helping me view the world in a more peaceful and immediate way, instead of looking to the future or past too often." (Rene)

Even if the therapist isn't a specialist in gender or transition, they need to be able to create a space for you to be open and honest so that you can explore your feelings and be able to manage what you're going through in a supportive way.

"Go with your instincts – if the counselling relationship doesn't feel right, just leave! You need trust for counselling to work. Our couples counsellor and personal counsellors (yes, we have three therapists between us, and it helps!) were all relatively unfamiliar with the subject but very attentive, non-judgmental and willing to do their homework. I would always go on recommendation. In the end, it's the quality of relationship that supports you to explore yourself that matters, not necessarily what the therapist knows, because no two trans people are the same. But I would expect a counsellor to recognise a need to develop their knowledge." (Ricky)

9

Loss and Grieving

Something that comes up in the forums and discussions is grief. In particular, this can be the grief of losing your partner as they start transition, or even grief when specific milestones are reached (for example, taking hormones, changing name or any sort of surgery).

> "Personally, I feel loss every day. Every day, I see my partner changing in front of my eyes. Mostly, it is only subtle changes, but even being as accepting to the situation [as] I am, I still will miss my 'man'." (Avril)

Let me preface this by saying that while I understand that every person and every situation is different, I don't understand the grief part. I cannot belittle how anyone else feels, and I can only speak for myself and my own experience.

> "It's never felt that way for me. I fell totally in love 20 years ago with a wonderful, sweet, sensitive, caring person who has been drifting away from me for years. We've been through some really tough patches, but that love and the belief that that person was still there on the inside made me hang on through them all, and now bit by bit they are coming back to me. She is the person that was always there on the inside; she's the person I fell in love with even though I had no idea at the time. I know what [being] married to

the wrong person feels like, I know I'm now married to the right person, [and] I'm not throwing that away." (Helen)

The theory behind grieving for a trans partner is that we are supposed to grieve the person that is being replaced, the former gender, the old name, the way things were.

"I haven't experienced this significantly, but I was not attached to my partner's identity as a woman, and so it's less relevant to me. I think any grief I've experienced could just be due to changes in his personality that were more subtle, but it's pretty negligible. I know a lot of other people experience this and have seen conversations through a friend's Facebook where her trans friends were actually triggered and upset by people claiming they had grief over their significant others coming out as trans. This is definitely something that deserves more attention so trans-identified partners can understand that their loved ones *also* are dealing with this huge thing happening in their lives, and they need to be a bit more generous and understanding about it. Conversely, the cisgender partners also need to understand their grief is normal and there is help for it." (Julia)

Some people feel strongly that this approach doesn't apply to them.

"I don't get that. To me, my wife is exactly the same person, just running on a different fuel, and it's as if you are grieving the weight that someone has lost when they go on a diet. It made them unhappy, and now they are working really hard to be a slimmer, happier person. How can you begrudge that? How must it make your partner feel if you are grieving who they once were? It's not as if they have a life-threatening illness; they aren't going anywhere." (Jo)

In my view, the things that made you love the person you are with are the things that make the person who they are. Yes, there are bound to be changes, but we all change as we age; we change jobs or even careers and we expect the world to be supportive. Perhaps it would be easier on us as partners if we viewed transition from the perspective that life changes are inevitable.

"We moved house recently, and the move itself was interesting for lots of reasons. Firstly, just having men around who were helping us move brought into sharp focus the difference between having men around and not. The male smell with all that testosterone was far from attractive to me, and there was so much of our stuff that was completely unfathomable to them, like my beautiful new coat stand shaped like a woman, our mugs that are bone china and painted by Natasha Law (who, as Wikipedia puts it, 'is known for her sexy line drawings which lie on the boundary between art and fashion. Her work also features strong and evident erotic undertones...' Ahem. Exactly).

I suppose it seals the deal; for me there is no turning back to hetero-land. It is more than just the mugs and the man-smell, though; it's the realisation as I saw everything that we have collected as we've built our life together [that] she is the one. The only one. And as much as we sometimes have our little spats, the reality is that fundamentally, deep down inside, we are connected. We are a single unit. The trans thing doesn't matter, the history doesn't matter, we are who we are. And we are better together.

I think the key message I would like to scream from the rooftops is that no matter how much she changes from the hormones, the voice training and all the other [things] that have happened and are due to happen, she is the same person. She is my person. And I love her to bits." (Jo)

You need to really analyse what you are mourning. You may not actually be mourning the person (because they are evidently there), but you may be mourning what you thought your life would be like. You may be mourning your identity in the context of the relationship; for example, you could mourn the idea of being a wife who is looked after by her husband or being a lesbian wife who's out defying straight norms.

"For me, there was a great deal of grief which it felt impossible to share with anyone. Each week brought a new small thing which felt like a sad loss. I found it particularly difficult when he had the skin taken from his left arm for the phalloplasty. It felt like the last bit of the body I had loved had been taken away from me." (Sasha)

Some people also find that they can take comfort in religion, but this is also not always done with a partner in mind.

"For me, there was a huge sense of loss which I have described with relation to the Christian naming ceremony my husband had.

Naming ceremonies provide a specific set of challenges, because they may have very different meanings for some of those present. Whilst my husband viewed his naming ceremony as a celebration and recommitment, I viewed it in many ways as a funeral. This was not easy for either of us, and I am sure it was also not easy for the very understanding and skilled minister leading the occasion, who was aware of the variety of feelings held by those in attendance at the evening service that night (which the naming ceremony occurred within).

The naming ceremony is a way to celebrate and allow the trans person to recommit themselves before God as they truly are. In doing this, there is an implicit formal acknowledgement of who they are not. It is this 'who they are not' that the partner initially got to know and fall in love with. It can be very difficult for the partner to get to the stage of feeling that those things were all secondary and the primary, ontological person remains the same. It is this final aspect which gets to the root of why I think it feels like a funeral service for the person who has been lost at the same time [as] being a celebration for the trans person of who they truly are." (Sally Rush)

I cannot stress enough that you need to look at precisely what it is that you are mourning, because it's only by understanding this that you will be able to get past the feelings of grief (which can be overwhelming sometimes) and get to acceptance.

"The thing that I found most bewildering about the grieving stages was that it proved to be possible to be simultaneously awash in grief for what I was losing and delighted with what I was gaining. I also could never predict what would hit me hardest; laser hair removal didn't bother me at all, but I cried for days when she threw out her men's underwear. I definitely had to mourn each change that I perceived as a loss, and we both had to accept that this was not something I could control. I would generally come to a point where I was at peace with the change, but I had to work through the grieving process first." (Tasha Martin)

For many people (especially people who identified as straight before the transition), the grief comes not from the actual person no longer being there, but is about belonging to the default heteronormative landscape.

"I mourned being straight, and I mourned having the world default to my relationship configuration. Being in a relationship with a trans person means that you are hardly ever represented in movies, television series or advertising. The implicit validation that we're normal is stripped away. I mourned having a relationship that was easy to explain.

> While I am completely, overwhelmingly supportive and in love with my wife, it's exhausting to correct every single assumed 'your husband' with 'my wife', especially when, in the beginning, not correcting feels like a betrayal. I mourned being 'normal'." (Jo)

Losing the privileges that come with being heterosexual can be hard on people, especially when they feel that they can no longer be as affectionate in public.

> "I have never felt a loss for my partner, as I don't feel they have gone. I do miss the traditional heterosexual activities, such as walking down the street holding hands without people staring." (Stevie)

Sometimes the mourning may be caused not by the loss of the relationship with a trans person, but actually because of the loss of a person's relationship with their unsupportive friends and family. Having to choose between a partner who is transitioning and family can also lead to complex feelings that are only indirectly linked to the transition.

> "My relationship with my family changed. I don't blame my wife at all for that; the cracks that appeared when my wife transitioned were undoubtedly there before even if I did not see them, but it all happened at the same time. It was exhausting to manage my wife and her feelings, cope with my family and their responses and figure out what this meant for our future." (Jo)

The grief associated with a person transitioning can also sometimes be because a person needs to let go of their long-held hopes and dreams. This doesn't mean the feelings are not valid, but it also doesn't mean that you should allow yourself to stay in that place; letting go of old hopes just makes way for you to build a new future together, unfettered by old expectations.

"There are moments when I grieve for the 'wife' I once had [and] the future I imagined with a woman who I planned on being a two-mum family with. Even now, two years since he came out and over ten months on testosterone, I struggle to look at pre-transition photos, especially our wedding photos. They are the biggest reminder that what I then wanted, hoped for and dreamed about is no longer reality. I am getting better at looking at them, but I know I have a long way to go until we can openly display those photos again. My reality now is much better; I love him more than I loved 'her', we are much closer as a couple, and I feel stronger in our relationship." (Anne)

Overcoming grief

Once you have looked at what exactly you're mourning, you can start to consider what that actually means to you and work on ways to overcome the grief. For me, this meant that I thought about what the benefits of transitioning were for us as a family.

"I feel that I am fortunate, so far, not to have felt any loss, as prior to my fling with my partner before he came out, I had only ever had relationships with men. I think because that fling had very negative effects on my health, I am just grateful that we have been able to come back from that place and that my partner is a much more well-adjusted, happier person now, having gone through some very tough times." (Rene)

People find that as their partners are happier in themselves, they can be happier as a couple. This doesn't mean that the dysphoria is magically gone; it means that because people start being seen as who they actually are, they are better able to take joy in the small moments.

"Transition brings about a lot of changes, yes, but it doesn't change who a person fundamentally is. If you love that person, and are open to the ways in which their transition will challenge your own beliefs, this can be a marvellous adventure. If it's your partner's body shape or genitals that you care about, well, that could be a problem, but I doubt that's the case for most people. In the end, it's been a privilege to see my partner become happier, calmer, more confident and more able to be loving. I'm so glad I did not sacrifice this amazing relationship for what I thought I knew about my own sexual orientation. We have also found ourselves in a much wider and more open, embracing community as a result of the changes we've been through. I'm happy for the changes this has brought me, despite the many challenges." (Ricky)

It can also be a time when you learn what is truly important to you, and the relationship and transition can be seen in a new light when compounded by significant life events.

"Our dog Lucy collapsed and died; comforting each other made us both realise that we are still soul mates and we cannot imagine life without each other." (Linda)

The thing that still takes my breath away is the strength of character in trans people when you take a solid look at what it means to be trans. No matter how much the world, the medical community or anyone else for that matter tries to tell them that they are wrong or that they shouldn't be authentic, trans people still step up. They remain steadfast in who they are; they have a strength of character that is undeniable, which taught me that I can be who I am. I too can have that strength of character. I can step forward and be seen.

That doesn't mean it is easy. It takes time, communication and lots of soul searching, but it does get better. You can get to a point where you recognise that the love that you share as a couple can completely overcome all obstacles. But that doesn't mean that you have to do it alone; seek out the people who've been there. Seek out other partners online and read articles, blogs and books by supportive partners. If you can find one, go to a mental health professional who has experience in dealing with partners of trans people. And keep communicating. Just keep communicating.

"Do not underestimate the grieving process, even if your relationship remains solid and happy. Ours has improved, if anything, but there were still huge losses. I don't personally feel I've lost a person, and I don't think it's fair to talk about it as if someone has died, because they haven't; they are right there with you, growing and changing, and they are the same person they always were as much as any of us is as we change through life.

Life is change. But it's still a powerful grieving process, because your life changes. People's perceptions of you and your partner change. You may face prejudice and at times rejection. You may face changes in your sex life, as dysphoria becomes more acute once acknowledged, or with hormonal changes and also because of surgery. You will see more of some people and less of others. You may start avoiding certain situations which were positive before – we stopped going to yoga class, for instance, because it became uncomfortable. You start worrying about the neighbours and stuff like that. It's a lot to process.

But, to be clear, I love my partner more and our relationship is better now I can see him clearly for who he is. He's a better person, more confident and more comfortable. Even though the whole process we've been through has at times been overwhelming for both of us, and that needs to be acknowledged, it's all been for the best. But sometimes, when something feels like a choice and a positive, we don't allow ourselves to acknowledge the difficult side or don't want people to see the hurt just in case they think it's all been a mistake.

It's *really* important to let yourself feel [overwhelmed along with] the grief and loss and upset and to have places to take the bad feelings. And, of course, you also have to tread a fine line with your partner – be real with them and not Polyanna-ish, but don't overburden them when you're struggling with it all. That's why support and counselling are so important." (Ricky)

10

Children, Fertility and Adoption

For trans people without children, the options for having children can be limited by where they are in transition. In the UK, being trans is not a barrier to adoption and fostering; however, the screening process can be very intrusive. It's important to think about what you'll tell future children about your partner's history, too.

> "We don't have children yet and are planning to adopt in ten or so years – we have our own personal reasons for wanting to adopt, but it's not related to us being transgender. Our children will grow up knowing about and respecting trans people, but we are undecided on whether/when we'd tell them we are transgender. I think I probably would when I felt they were mature enough to understand and not out me, but My Love is undecided on coming out to them or not." (Shae)

In trans women and other trans people who were assigned male at birth, taking estradiol suppresses the hormones needed to produce sperm, leading to a loss in fertility (NHS North of Tyne Area Prescribing Committee, 2016a). The timelines for potential infertility vary based on the person's genetics, their fertility before treatment and how long they have been taking the feminising hormones. Although some studies have shown that stopping hormone treatments may enable the testes to recover and start producing sperm again (World Professional Association for Transgender Health, 2011), for people who may want to have biological children it is advised that sperm storage be done prior to the start of hormone therapy (NHS North of Tyne Area Prescribing Committee, 2016a; World Professional Association for Transgender Health, 2011).

It is possible for trans men and other trans people who were assigned female at birth to get pregnant and carry a child. There are a few considerations which will make the process more complicated. The general fertility factors that influence a cis woman's chances of getting pregnant will also influence the trans person:

- age: after the age of 32, the ability for a person to get pregnant without medical assistance falls

- general health: some conditions can make it more difficult to get pregnant, such as endometriosis, polycystic ovarian syndrome, cancer treatment and some medications

- lifestyle factors: such as smoking, alcohol consumption and drug use.

For someone who is on testosterone and looking to get pregnant, it is generally advised to stop taking testosterone and get a full checkup (including hormone level checks) by a GP.

Even when it is medically possible to get pregnant, there are nevertheless substantial things to consider. It is very likely that the trans person is going to have significant dysphoria in the process of getting pregnant (especially if medical intervention is required), through the pregnancy or around childbirth. The medical establishment (and society in general) views pregnancy as a purely female process, so the likelihood of medical professionals misgendering a pregnant person as female is very high. There is also a chance that they will get treated differently, and they may also be seen as an anomaly and thus the focus of either interest or hostility. UK law is also not set up to deal with trans people having children, as a trans person who gives birth to a child will be listed on the birth certificate as the child's mother.

Where medical intervention is required (such as in-vitro fertilisation), it can be very costly if it is not approved by the NHS, and it is subject to very long waiting lists even if approved.

As an alternative, I suggest adoption. Although there are very few cases of trans people becoming foster parents or adopting children, there are no specific barriers. The adoption and fostering service cannot turn you down purely because you are trans or in a same-sex relationship, and not being married is also not a barrier; you may just need to approach multiple adoption agencies and find the one that you are most comfortable with and then be patient with them if they have not had experience of dealing with trans parents.

Part 2

TRANSITION

11

Social Transition

Social transition is the term I use to cover some of the aspects of transitioning that are not part of medical transitioning. This is also known as the Real-Life Experience. This section is largely a primer on some of the ways that trans people manage dysphoria and is by no means exhaustive.

Not all the sections will apply to your situation, and some may apply for a while and then no longer be relevant if your partner chooses to go through medical transitioning. It is worth noting that, for some medical interventions, a level of social transition may be required.

> "The Real-Life Experience was generally okay for my husband. Indeed, he was able to go through having a really good set of experiences, apart from some insults and the odd attack in a toilet (which is actually good going)." (Sally Rush)

Hair removal

Hair removal, especially facial hair removal, can be one of the longest and costliest processes to go through for trans women and trans feminine people. However, once you start the hair removal process, it will need to be done consistently for best results.

Laser/intense pulsed light (IPL) hair removal

Laser and IPL are distinct but similar approaches to hair removal. They use different technologies; however, the application and use are similar. These methods are only suitable for people who have pale skin and darker hair.

Laser and IPL involve placing a wand on the skin, and a light (either the intense pulsed light or the laser) uses the colour in the hair (melanin) to travel down to the root of the hair to damage it. Dark skin increases the risk of skin damage and also makes the treatment less effective. Another downside to this type of hair removal is that immediately after each treatment session the skin will appear irritated and the hair may appear darker until it falls out (usually within a few days, depending on the growth cycle and the effectiveness of the treatment).

The treatments are more expensive in the short term than electrolysis but can be very effective when trying to clear large patches of dark facial hair, which is very visible on lighter skin. Once you have completed a number of sessions of laser/IPL, it may be necessary to have electrolysis to remove any light-coloured hairs which the treatment may have missed.

Electrolysis

Electrolysis is a far more time-consuming treatment, although it is more cost effective in the short term. Electrolysis is suitable for most skin types, but the technician will insist that you do a patch test to check your skin's reaction to it.

Electrolysis involves inserting a very fine needle down the hair follicle and delivering a tiny electric shock to the root of the hair. The hair is then pulled out with tweezers. This means that while the skin may appear irritated immediately after the treatments, the hair is removed, which can make this a preferred option. The downside to electrolysis is that there is a limit on the length of the treatment session (based on your skin's reaction and the individual technician), which means that even small areas that have a lot of hair may require a number of sessions.

Epilators

An epilator is a small hand-held device (about the size of a cordless razor) that has a rotating set of tweezers that pull the hair out of the hair follicle. While this is not recommended for areas that have a lot of dense hair, and it is not a permanent hair removal solution, it can be very useful for removal of body hair. This is particularly helpful because the hair is removed rather than shaved and the frequency of use reduces over time as the hair thins out.

Clothes shopping

The best tip I can offer for clothes shopping is to buy a tape measure and help your partner take measurements of their body. Online shopping can be the simplest way to shop for clothes, but because the size ranges inevitably vary based on brand and cut, it's useful to have a set of measurements. It's also important to make sure the shop (whether online or on the high street) has a reasonable returns policy.

> "I found it useful to go clothes shopping with my husband, and whilst he developed his style, I was able to help discuss what I thought would work. This also helped me know his style, so if I were shopping alone for him, I would be more likely to get it right (e.g. at Christmas)." (Sally Rush)

Buying bras

This section is specifically for trans women and trans feminine people. The breast binding section discusses options for trans men and trans masculine people.

The ability to have breasts that appear natural can be very important to people who have dysphoria about not having enough breast tissue. Often, a bra fitting at a specialist shop is not available to trans people, as it may be dysphoric or even turn unpleasant if the person doing the fitting is unfamiliar with trans people or insensitive to what they need. If your partner has just started hormones it is better to get one or two bras that fit well as they may need to be replaced as their breasts develop and change shape.

Something I found helpful was to buy post-surgery bras, which have a pocket in the cup that keep the prosthetic breasts or fillers in place.

Memory foam bras have soft cups that mould to a person's breast shape, so for people whose breasts are developing this allows for a smooth and even look and allows for more growth than a traditional foam push up bra. Bras that have small pockets with inserts that can be removed as a person's breast shape changes and grows are also useful.

Breast binding

Breast binding is a way to flatten the breast tissue to create a more masculinised chest. It is important to make sure that binding is done safely, because it can have a serious impact on health if it is done wrong. Never use bandages, duct tape or cling film as an alternative to a binder. If a binder isn't an option, try using a sports bra or a compression vest, but it is important to get the correct size.

Voice coaching

Voice coaching can be very expensive and difficult to find. There are, however, a lot of online videos which can give hints and tips about how to achieve gradual changes in a person's voice. The key that makes voice coaching effective is practice;

you can get the best voice coach, but they will still only be able to give you advice, and the effectiveness will come down to practice.

Genital tucking

Genital tucking refers to placing the penis and testes between the legs in order to create a flat front. Tucking can be incredibly important not just to manage dysphoria but also for safety, as for trans women and trans feminine people someone finding out they are trans can put them at risk of violence.

Tucking can have an impact on fertility (as it doesn't allow the testes to keep cooler than the rest of the body), so if this is an issue, it is often suggested that the person banks sperm and tucks sparingly. As an alternative to the specialist gaffs (tucking devices) or tape that are commonly suggested, a set of shaping knickers (also known as control underwear) could be used.

Packing

Packing refers to using a penile prosthesis to give the appearance of having a penis. There are a number of packing straps and types of speciality underwear available that will assist with keeping the prosthetic in place.

12

Medical Transitioning

"Being trans is quite a selfish transition. I found that there has been an expectation (either conscious or subconscious) that I need to be strong for my wife or okay with things that her family are struggling with. The Distinction group has really helped me, as I have been able to read about similar issues that others are going through and provide support to those in earlier stages." (Stevie)

This section will follow the medical model for transitioning as defined by WPATH, which is the leading organisation that deals with trans healthcare. The WPATH Standards of Care are the guide for medical professionals to use when treating trans and gender nonconforming patients (World Professional Association for Transgender Health, 2011).

Bear in mind that these are the guidelines published by and for medical professionals, and, as such, they are a broad-strokes view of what may apply to most trans people. This doesn't mean that all the steps will be relevant to your situation. As people are becoming more accepting and open to different gender expressions, the approach is becoming a lot more tailored to the individual rather than a rigid process dictated by the medical profession, with the key aim being to ease the dysphoria and make a person more comfortable in their identity. The next section will cover the various options available to trans people, but it must be noted that a lot of the information and treatments are aimed specifically at binary trans people (trans men or trans women). The treatment and options for non-binary people can vary greatly based on the person's dysphoria and treatment that they choose, but also based on ignorance by many clinicians and gender specialists as to the appropriate course of action.

> "My partner is the first FTM to undergo treatment in our area. It's taken a lot of research, but our GP surgery has been supportive and is now taking a lead role." (Nicola Kalisky)

Attending appointments with your partner

For a person who wants to support a trans partner through transition, the subject of attending the medical appointments with them can be complex. Some trans people will want their partner to be there to support them, and some people won't. Both opinions are valid, and it's important to respect your partner's decision if they choose not to have you at the appointment. The initial clinician that a trans person will see is usually a psychiatrist or a mental health professional, so there may be a number of topics that someone may want to keep private. It could also be that the trans person doesn't want the clinician to see them as being influenced by their partner.

> "The first relates to seeing the GP and then the local specialist. It helped that my husband's minister was also a trained GP, and so she had talked through a lot of hard questions he would face beforehand. Additionally, he is a science geek and had read a range of science papers as well as being used to talking to people of that level of education on an equal level. This all helped. With his own GP, using the research he had done beforehand, he was able to talk through the process and what he needed in terms of a referral. When that came through, he was able to talk to the local trust's psychiatrist in an appropriate way, explaining in detail what was going on. The only problem here was

being told from that point on that it was very surprising I was still with him." (Sally Rush)

If you do attend the clinician appointments, you may be ignored by your partner and the clinician. Often, clinicians will have their office set up specifically so that anyone who attends with their patients is not included in the discussion. This is the time that the clinician needs to get to know the patient, and they need to get as full a picture of the individual as they can without outside influence. Your partner will be more focused on making sure they give the clinician a complete picture of their dysphoria in the shortest amount of time so that they can further their treatment as quickly as possible.

"We had to use the private route – I found the details – because we had been told by the only trans person we knew to go to see a private clinician; I gave the contact details to my partner to make the appointment. She was so happy; we went a few weeks later, together. We walked into the clinician's room, and I was sat in a corner and I was excluded. It was made perfectly clear; it was nothing to do with me. When we left the room, I said I was not happy, and my partner suggested that I did not go in with her again." (Linda)

A compromise may be to go with your partner to the appointment but wait in the waiting room so that they can both be supported and allowed the privacy that they need to speak freely with the clinician.

Seeking medical intervention

The first step in the medical transition is to get a referral to a gender specialist.

"People were what we now call trans before medicine came along to help us. It's important we don't let medical procedures define who we are, even if they help us." (Ricky)

Specialists vary by country. In the UK, you can self-refer to a specialist if you go privately, but you will need to get a referral from your GP if you go through the National Health Service (NHS). In order to rule out gender dysphoria as a symptom of other issues, the clinician will then assess the person's gender dysphoria by looking at a number of factors (as dictated by WPATH):

- a person's history of gender dysphoria and how it developed: this is typically done by asking when the person first knew that they are trans

- how this feeling of being trans has impacted on their mental health

- how much support the person has, in terms of family, friends and peers (both in person and online)

- what contact or groups the person is involved with regarding gender dysphoria

- any other relevant medical conditions that may impact the person's gender dysphoria or treatment options.

"The GIC gave him some different experiences. He was wary of the life story he was telling, knowing there seemed to be some kind of accepted narrative. I was certainly not in the expected narrative [that] one doctor there expected. She told my husband I would leave him. The other professional he saw was much better." (Sally Rush)

The clinician should also, either in the initial consultation or a follow-up meeting, provide information regarding what the different options are to alleviate gender dysphoria. This can also include discussing what the implications are of changing a person's gender role, especially if these are long-term impacts from options such as surgery. Where necessary, the clinician will also refer the person to mental health professionals or groups that can provide support and also discuss how to treat co-existing mental health concerns.

Once the clinician has confirmed a diagnosis of gender dysphoria, and if the patient chooses to do so, they will assess and prepare the person for hormone therapy. Based on individual factors and on clinic guidelines, this is usually more than six months after the patient's first appointment. This process of confirming a person's diagnosis will need to be done with each clinician they see in the process, which can become very frustrating.

"Transitioning medically involves *a lot* of annoying repetition, and the onus is on the trans person to prove their 'transness' in a way that continues to astound me. I have chronic pain, and I've not had to relentlessly prove it, or keep a pain diary, or fill out several questionnaires about what pain was like in my house when I was young, how my mum dealt with pain, when did I first realise I might be someone who struggled with pain, etc., etc. I just went to my GP, described the pain, and was believed. But if you have gender dysphoria, you have to endlessly get up and do what we call 'the trans dance', which we sing to the tune of 'The Time Warp' from *Rocky Horror* (it helps). So far, and this is pre-GIC, he's had to describe his 'transness' to his GP, then the NHS psychologist the GP sent him to, then the counselling service, then three times more to various other services to get his bridging script for testosterone! *And* we've just found out his first GIC appointment will be yet another psychologist evaluation so he can say all the stuff that's surely already on his notes! 'Let's Do the Trans Dance Again!!!'" (Josephine Humphrey)

There is, however, a glaring lack of discussion and support for partners in the process.

> "The clinicians have made it perfectly clear to my partner and [me that] spouses are not welcome; my partner is special, and they will look after her." (Linda)

Hormones

Starting hormones can be one of the difficult junctures in a relationship with a trans person. This is because there is often a disconnect between what the trans person feels and what their partner is going through.

Because of the long waiting lists and the lengthy procedures that need to be followed before getting hormones, by the time they get a prescription and start taking hormones, trans people may be feeling elated. They may feel that they have official medical recognition for being trans, they may feel like their transition process is actually starting, they may feel like they are finally "running on the correct fuel" and that finally their bodies will match with their gender identity.

For partners, however, this can be a difficult time, because while you may feel happy for your partner finally being able to get what they need, you may also start worrying about what changes the hormones will bring. These worries do not take away from the fact that you want the relationship to continue, but actually may be because you are afraid that your partner's changes will cause the relationship to change.

The thing to remember about hormones is that it takes a long time to change a person, and the effects are subtle. It's not as if you'll wake up next to a completely different person one morning. There will be enough time for you to get used to each change on its own.

> "I remember being absolutely terrified of my partner taking hormones. He had a tendency to be grumpy, especially

at certain times of the month, and I assumed he would become aggressive on T. How wrong I was! He is so much calmer, and the only times he is grumpy these days is when his T shot is due. I've now learned the link between T and aggression is pretty tenuous, so don't let guys ever get away with saying 'the T made me do it'. The changes on T were very gradual, but my partner is completely read as a man now (two years on T). He is quite hairy, which I like more than he does! The changes are subtle; it's interesting. I look at old photos and still see the same person. It's quite fun watching things change. I would say he's more the same than different, though." (Ricky)

There are a few things that could help you manage when your partner is starting hormones:

- Put away any pictures of your partner that you have around the house. That way, you won't have a constant reminder of how different they are.

- Think about what scares you the most about them taking hormones. Try to be specific; rather than "you'll be a different person", try "I'm afraid you won't listen to me any more" or "I'm afraid I won't find you attractive."

- Talk to your partner about the specifics and come up with strategies to make sure that your fears are addressed; for example, schedule time to talk (I am a great advocate for going for a walk to talk about what's going on).

Once your partner has started taking hormones, the challenges change. While the slow progress will give you comfort, this gradual progress can be a big challenge for trans people. Most don't believe that hormones will change them overnight, and taking hormones won't eliminate the feelings of dysphoria. Alternatively, when the changes do start and your partner starts noticing their body changing, your original fears could return.

It's important to take a step back and make sure you use the strategies that you came up with – for example, the long walks to talk.

Criteria for getting hormone therapy

It's the clinician's responsibility to make sure the person is ready for hormone therapy and fully understands the implications. This will usually mean that the person has told their family and community and that any medical risks have been taken into consideration. If the person is of reproductive age, the clinician may also choose to discuss the options for future fertility.

If a person has gone private, a referral letter may be required (especially where the referral is from a clinician who does not provide prescriptions). The referral letter for hormone therapy will include the following information:

- name and identification
- the diagnosis
- the clinician's relationship to the patient (for example, how long the clinician has been seeing the patient)
- an explanation that the criteria for the hormone referral have been met
- a statement that includes the consent of the patient
- the details of the clinician.

If, however, the referral is made within a gender clinic, this information will be noted in the person's file and then passed to the relevant clinician.

The WPATH Standards of Care (World Professional Association for Transgender Health, 2011) describe the criteria for getting a prescription for hormone therapy, but these are guidelines, and each case should be looked at on an individual level. Nevertheless, the onus is on the clinician to discuss the options with the person and make sure there is mutual understanding on the reasons for prescribing (or delaying the prescription).

The Standards of Care list the following requirements for hormone therapy.

Gender dysphoria which is consistent (i.e. hasn't gone away) and well documented

This usually means that a patient has to explain how they experience gender dysphoria and also needs to provide details of when they first noticed it, how it's impacted them and how long they've had it for.

Patient's age

The person must be old enough to consent to treatment. In the UK, this age is 16, but parental consent can be given for someone younger; however, different standard of care guidelines have been issued by WPATH for young people who have gender dysphoria.

Capacity to consent for treatment

The clinician will need to ensure that the person has the ability to understand the treatment and is able to adequately communicate their decision. This is standard with most medical procedures, and the clinician will be looking for any impairment of the person making the decision. Physicians look for such things as:

- intoxication (through drugs or alcohol)

- severe learning disabilities

- brain damage or any other relevant physical or mental conditions

- certain mental health conditions (such as schizophrenia or bipolar disorder).

If significant medical or mental concerns are present, they must be reasonably well controlled

If a person does have mental health or other medical concerns, the clinician will need to be comfortable that the person has these under control prior to prescribing hormones. This is done so that the effects of the hormones on these conditions can be monitored and, if necessary, the hormones changed.

Bridging hormones

> "I think there needs to be more information about bridging hormones and how to access them. It may also be worth covering how excruciating the wait is before you even get to see a medical professional at the GIC, let alone how long it takes before they get any treatment." (Avril)

In the UK, it's a GP's responsibility to refer a person to one of the GICs to see a gender specialist as soon as possible. There is no longer a requirement to have a psychiatric or psychological assessment done before the referral. Given that the waiting time to get the initial appointment at a GIC is 42 weeks and rising (UK Trans Info, 2016), the General Medical Council have recognised that this may cause significant harm to trans people and have provided guidance to GPs that they may, after consulting a gender specialist, prescribe bridging hormones to reduce the risks to the person's mental health and prevent the person going online to buy hormones from an unregulated source. The restrictions on getting these bridging hormones can actually be a substantial barrier, though, because *all* the following criteria need to be met:

a. the patient is already self-prescribing with hormones obtained from an unregulated source (over the internet or otherwise on the black market)

b. the bridging prescription is intended to mitigate a risk of self-harm or suicide

c. the doctor has sought the advice of a gender specialist and prescribes the lowest acceptable dose in the circumstances.

(General Medical Council UK, 2016)

Due to the complications that people need to deal with to get treatment, some people choose to self-medicate. There are serious risks associated with self-medicating, primarily with regards to harm from the wrong dosage, side effects or ignoring contraindications of hormones. In addition, the illegally obtained medications may not even contain the listed hormones/dosages or be otherwise unsafe to take. Unfortunately, there is no way to be sure that medications bought online from unregulated providers are what they are advertised to be.

Masculinising hormones

Masculine hormones are required by trans men and some non-binary people in order to change their secondary sexual characteristics (such as facial hair and deepening of the voice).

"My Love was already on testosterone for a year when we met, and it's now been over two and a half years. Most of his changes were already complete by then, or they seem to be, to me. I love the little scruff (beard) he gets, though he's unhappy with it being a smidge patchy in places. I've seen a couple of 'before' photos, and I'm very attracted to how masculine his features have become. I don't know what his lower area was like before testosterone, but the growth he'd had was good, and I never thought of it as gendered; but, if I had to, I would have definitely seen it as male, because he's male, and it had been affected by the testosterone, which was helpful during intimacy.

All in all, I've always been attracted to his body, and I definitely see it as masculine, which I'm sure was mostly or all down to the testosterone." (Shae)

Blood tests

It's usual that a clinician will require a set of baseline blood tests to determine a person's hormone levels before they start on cross-sex hormones (see NHS North of Tyne Area Prescribing Committee, 2016b). These blood tests are available from the GP and would ordinarily include:

- blood pressure

- full blood count

- urea and electrolytes

- liver function

- fasting blood glucose or HbA1C

- lipid profile

- thyroid function

- serum testosterone

- estradiol

- prolactin, LH and FSH.

A pregnancy test is also usually recommended if there is any risk of being pregnant.

Once the person has started using hormones, blood pressure and hormone levels will then be regularly monitored to ensure that there are no significant medical concerns and that the treatment is working. The regularity of these tests can vary from every three months up to every six months. It is typical for the clinician at the GIC to request a blood test prior to or immediately after each appointment.

The monitoring blood tests will usually be the same as the previous tests, with the exception of the thyroid panel and pregnancy test.

It's important to note that the time that a person takes their hormones can influence the blood test. As a result, it's usually advised for people using injections that the tests be administered just before taking the next injection. The serum testosterone level that is usually aimed for is toward the lower end of the male reference range (8–12 nmol/L) (NHS North of Tyne Area Prescribing Committee, 2016b). If the person is using a topical gel, the blood tests should be taken between four and six hours since the last dose was applied, which means that the goal for the serum testosterone level is the middle of the male reference range (15–20 nmol/L) (NHS North of Tyne Area Prescribing Committee, 2016b).

Once the ideal levels have been reached, the monitoring blood tests will go down to approximately once every six months for the first three years. After that, blood tests will likely be only once a year. As the person ages, a small drop in testosterone is considered normal, but as with everything in this section, this should be discussed and agreed with the clinician.

Types of testosterone

There are different types of testosterone available, and which one is prescribed is based on medical history and the clinician's recommendation. The two most widely used types of masculinising treatment are:

- testosterone injection

- testosterone topical gel.

TESTOSTERONE INJECTION

The types of injections typically prescribed are:

- Nebido, given roughly every 10 to 20 weeks

- Sustanon, usually every two to six weeks

- Testosterone Enantate, not usually prescribed, but it would also be every two to six weeks.

The key positive with injected testosterone is that there is less upkeep required, because there is no daily administration such as is required by the topical gel.

The downside to the testosterone injections is that fine-tuning of a dosage is more difficult to achieve, since it is a single dose that lasts several weeks. In addition, if you have an allergy to any of the ingredients, you will obviously not be able to continue with the injection and will be switched to a topical testosterone gel.

TESTOSTERONE TOPICAL GEL

The types of topical applications of testosterone are:

- Testogel
- Tostran
- Testim.

All the topical applications are used daily, which will allow the clinician to adjust the dosage of testosterone to get the correct results. If a person chooses to take a lower dose of testosterone to reduce the masculinising effects, the clinician will usually recommend one of the above topical applications.

The key downside to the topical application is that the person taking the testosterone will need to be careful not to transfer the testosterone to anyone else in the household by coming into contact immediately after applying the gel.

> "In terms of the impact of hormones on me, they impacted in practical ways of my husband and I not being able to shower together any more, and we have to make sure he uses a separate towel all the time. With regard to sex, we need to make sure that there has been enough time since he put it on for the gel to have absorbed, or else we have to make love before he goes for his shower and starts his morning routine." (Sally Rush)

Effects of testosterone

"The first month of testosterone made my husband moodier and more aggressive, which we knew to expect. It was hard to deal with; I had said to him if it gets too much for me, he would have to move out to his mother's house for a while, but it thankfully never got to that point. He recognised the signs and learnt to handle the mood swings that came with HRT." (Anne)

The following information from the NHS North of Tyne Area Prescribing Committee (2016b) shows what effects can be expected when a person is taking testosterone and the likely time scales. These effects are largely dependent on a number of factors, such as the person's hormone levels, age, genetic makeup and general health. If the person isn't getting the results that they are looking for, consult with the clinician to what options are available to assist.

- Expected to start around one to six months:

  - skin oiliness/acne – expected to stabilise after one to two years.

- Expected to start around two to six months:

  - cessation of periods.

- Expected to start around three to six months:

  - growth of facial and body hair – expected maximum effect is between three and five years

  - body fat redistribution – expected maximum effect is between two and five years

  - clitoral enlargement – expected maximum effect is between one and two years

  - vaginal atrophy – expected maximum effect is between one and two years.

- Expected to start around three to twelve months:

  - deepened voice – expected maximum effect is between one and two years.

- Expected to start around six to twelve months:

  - increased strength and muscle mass – expected maximum effect is between two and five years.

STOPPING PERIODS

If the testosterone treatment doesn't stop the periods (and this causes an issue due to gender dysphoria), there are ovarian suppression medications available (known as gonadotropin-releasing hormone analogue [or GnRH-a]) in the form of an implant once every four weeks (NHS North of Tyne Area Prescribing Committee 2016b). It's important to note that GnRH-a stops ovarian function and will only be given if the clinician is satisfied that the testosterone levels are stable. Introduction of GnRH-a will also impact the time scales for the effects of testosterone.

Risks of masculinising hormones

As with all types of medical treatments, there are possible risks for people taking testosterone. These increased risks are why the blood tests are taken regularly, so that the clinician can make sure that complications are identified and dealt with early.

- There is a likely increased risk of:

  - polycythaemia (a rare blood condition) – associated with serum testosterone levels above the reference male range

  - weight gain/increased visceral fat

  - acne

  - androgenic alopecia (balding)

  - sleep apnoea.

- There is a possible increased risk of:

  - altered lipid profiles (the amount and types of fats in the body) – people who are on testosterone who also have polycystic ovarian syndrome may also be at greater risk of this developing

  - liver dysfunction.

- There is a possible increased risk, with the presence of additional risk factors, of:

  - type 2 diabetes – people who are on testosterone who also have polycystic ovarian syndrome may also be at greater risk of this developing

  - hypertension – people who are on testosterone who also have polycystic ovarian syndrome may also be at greater risk of this developing

  - mania and psychosis in patients with pre-existing disorders – also associated with serum testosterone above the reference male range

  - cardiovascular disease.

- There is no increased risk or inconclusive evidence of a change in risk of developing:

  - breast cancer

  - osteoporosis

  - cervical cancer

  - ovarian cancer

  - uterine cancer.

    (NHS North of Tyne Area Prescribing Committee, 2016b)

Feminising hormones

Feminine hormones are required by trans women and some non-binary people in order to suppress the effects of naturally produced testosterone and enable changes to their secondary sexual characteristics (such as breast development and softening of skin).

"I was actually eager for her to start hormones, because I did and do prefer women physically. HRT also made her calmer, more relaxed, more resilient and sometimes more cheerful, all of which were nice changes. In terms of physical changes, HRT for trans women has the same general results as puberty for a cis girl (softer skin, breast growth, curves from fat distributing to mature female locations, etc.). We were both somewhat surprised by how fast some of those changes happened, but it was a pleasant surprise. That first year included a lot of bra shopping and clothes shopping (for the first time, she actually enjoyed finding clothes!). Personally, I was startled and delighted by how pretty she became, and how quickly it was impossible for me to look at her and see the ghost of my husband. That helped a lot; I may be an outlier in that respect, but the hardest part of transition was losing my husband and being haunted by the memories of what I'd given up. Rationally, I knew that she wasn't gone and hadn't even changed all that much, but emotionally, I was still grieving. For whatever reason, when she and I both began to see the woman she was physically becoming, I was also able to perceive the payoff for toughing it out through the early days of transition."
(Tasha Martin)

Blood tests

The clinician will usually require a set of baseline blood tests to determine a person's hormone levels before they start on hormones. These blood tests are available from the GP and would ordinarily include:

- full blood count

- urea and electrolytes

- liver function

- fasting blood glucose or HbA1C

- lipid profile

- thyroid function

- serum testosterone

- serum estradiol

- serum prolactin

- LH and FSH.

In addition to blood tests, the following will also be monitored:

- blood pressure

- body mass index.

Once the person has started using hormones, blood pressure and hormone level tests will then be regularly repeated to ensure that there are no significant medical concerns and that the treatment is working. The regularity of these tests can vary from every three months up to every six months. It is typical for the clinician at the GIC to request a blood test prior to or immediately after each appointment.

Based on the type of oestrogen that is being taken, the timing of the blood tests is important to get an accurate result. For people who are taking tablets, the blood tests should be taken 24 hours after a dose; it should be 48 hours after a new patch has been applied and between four and six hours after the gel has been applied (NHS North of Tyne Area Prescribing Committee, 2016a). The levels of hormones on oestrogen treatment are expected to be in the upper half or upper third of the reference female range.

Once the ideal levels have been reached, the monitoring blood tests will go down to approximately once every six months for the first three years. After this, it's expected that blood tests are only needed once a year.

Types of hormones prescribed
ESTRADIOL

Estradiol is a form of oestrogen. The estradiol that is effective for trans people is estradiol valerate, which may be exchanged by the pharmacist when a prescription is collected, so it's worth making sure you are getting the correct one.

Estradiol is given in three forms:

- tablet – taken daily

- transdermal patch – changed twice a week

- gel – applied daily.

Implants are very rarely given, as it is difficult to monitor and adjust the hormone levels, since they are replaced between four and eight months.

There is a current shortage of injectable estradiol valerate, and pills may use different esters of estradiol (such as cypionate). Patches and gels generally use estradiol, not an ester, because they skip the first pass through the liver wherein the ester would be broken down into estradiol. Gels and patches are preferred for people who are smokers or are at higher risk of liver disease or thrombosis (blood clots).

The prescription for estradiol is usually started at a lower dosage and increased based on blood tests taken regularly until the required levels are reached. These will need to be reviewed if a person is also prescribed testosterone blockers and after genital surgery, because both of these can have an impact on the amount of hormones in the body.

TESTOSTERONE BLOCKERS

GnRH-a is a hormone that suppresses testosterone so that the maximum results of the estradiol therapy can be achieved, although it is often added after estradiol is prescribed. GnRH-a can be given in the following forms:

- Goserelin – a low-dose implant given every four weeks; if there are no issues, a higher dosage is given every 12 weeks.

- Tripterelin (also known as Decapeptyl, Gonapeptyl) – an injection is given every four weeks.

- Leuprorelin (also known as Prostap, Lutrate) – an injection is given every four weeks.

A side effect of GnRH-a is that there is a period where the testosterone in the body flares up following the injection, and this can cause several mental health and behavioural effects, such as increased irritability and increase in risky behaviour. This effect only lasts a few days, but it's important to discuss the possible preventions with your clinician, as there are medications that can assist in the short term (such as Cyprotene, discussed in the next section).

> "When my wife first started on the testosterone blocker injections, no one warned us about the testosterone spike that happens for the first few days after the injection, and the GP didn't give us any of those short-term blockers to counteract the effects. She was in a stressful time at work already, and the day after getting the injection, she yelled at her boss, walked out of work and got fired. She was completely devastated by the whole thing, and we couldn't understand what had happened. It was only months later that a fellow trans woman mentioned that she gets the tablets that prevent the spike, but of course, by then, the damage had been done." (Jo)

GnRH-a must be taken with another hormone (such as estradiol or testosterone) to prevent hypogonadism (where the body has neither masculine nor feminine hormones), which can cause side effects such as hot flushes, depression, lowered libido, reduced height (in young people), loss of muscle and osteoporosis (NHS North of Tyne Area Prescribing Committee, 2016a).

OTHER AVAILABLE ANTI-ANDROGEN TREATMENTS

There are other medications which may be required in addition to estradiol and/or GnRH-a, but these will only be prescribed if there is a specific reason. It is worth discussing your need for these with your clinician. These are:

- Finasteride – this is a tablet taken daily which blocks the body's processing of testosterone and can stop male pattern baldness and some body hair growth. This is usually only prescribed in the short term, until GnRH-a is started.

- Cyprotene – this is a tablet taken daily which prevents the spike in testosterone caused by the GnRH-a injection.

- Spironolactone – this is a pill to reduce water retention in patients with high blood pressure or heart conditions, but is the most common anti-androgen prescribed in the US.

Effects of feminising hormones

The effects of feminising hormones are based on an individual person's body, how quickly the right dosage of estradiol is achieved and whether testosterone blockers are prescribed. This can also be impacted by the person's age, genetic makeup and general health.

"Hormones made my partner act a little bit like an overemotional teenager. She would be angry one moment, crying the next and then absolutely fine – all in a short period of time. It also made her react to situations in weird ways...crying over toast burning, etc." (Stevie)

If the person isn't getting the results that they are looking for, consult with the clinician as to what options are available to assist.

- Expected to start around one to three months:
  - decreased libido – expected to stabilise after one to two years
  - decreased spontaneous erections – expected maximum effect is between three and six months
  - male pattern baldness – hair loss stops in one to three months, but there is no regrowth of hair that has previously been lost. Expected maximum effect is between one and two years.

- Expected to start around three to six months:
  - body fat redistribution – expected maximum effect is between two and five years
  - decreased muscle mass/strength – expected maximum effect is between one and two years
  - softening of skin/decreased oiliness
  - breast growth – expected maximum effect is between two and three years
  - decreased testicular volume – expected maximum effect is between two and three years.

- Expected to start around six to twelve months:
  - thinning and slowed growth of body and facial hair – expected maximum effect is three years.

- The following effects are dependent on the individual:

  - sexual dysfunction

  - decreased sperm production.

Risks of feminising hormones

As with all types of medical treatments, there are possible risks for people taking feminising hormones (see NHS North of Tyne Area Prescribing Committee, 2016a). These increased risks are why the blood tests are taken regularly, so that the clinician can make sure that any complications are identified and dealt with early.

- There is a likely increased risk of:

  - venous thromboembolic disease (usually a higher risk with tablets than with gel or transdermal patches)

  - gallstones

  - elevated liver enzymes

  - weight gain

  - hypertriglyceridemia (increased amount of fatty molecules in the blood).

- There is a likely increased risk, with presence of additional risk factors, of:

  - cardiovascular disease.

- There is a possible increased risk of:

  - hypertension (high blood pressure)

  - hyperprolactinemia or prolactinoma.

- There is a possible increased risk, with presence of additional risk factors, of:

  - type 2 diabetes.

- There is no increased risk or inconclusive evidence of a change in risk of developing:

  – breast cancer.

FEMINISING HORMONES AND SURGERY

Because of the increased risks of venous thromboembolism from feminising hormones, it is recommended that estradiol be stopped between four and six weeks before any kind of surgery where a person will be immobilised afterward, including genital surgery.

Post-surgery testosterone

If a trans person has had the testes removed, they may suffer from a decreased libido. In these cases, it is often recommended that a low dose of testosterone is taken to rectify this. The dose of testosterone administered is equivalent to what is prescribed to cisgender women for libido issues, and it is closely monitored to ensure that the dose is sufficient to combat the low libido but not high enough to introduce the masculinising effects of testosterone. Because of the need to monitor the dosage carefully, a topical gel is often recommended, such as:

- Testogel

- Tostran

- Testim.

However, some trans people may find using testosterone dysphoric.

Progesterone

Progesterone (a hormone which works alongside oestrogen in the ovulation cycle) is not generally offered in the UK (although it is included in the hormone regime in some countries). Some trans people on feminising hormones sometimes feel that they should also be taking progesterone, because they feel that it may assist with breast development and have other psychological impacts. This is, however, a myth (Curtis, 2009); in fact, progesterone can inhibit breast growth.

Progesterone is produced in the adrenal glands of a person (irrespective of gender) and is a precursor to testosterone (this includes both progesterone produced by the body as well as that taken as medication). An example of this is progesterone-only contraceptives, which reduce the effects of oestrogen and thus prevent the person from getting pregnant. Progesterone actually reduces the feminisation effects of oestrogen in the following ways:

- If a person is taking estradiol tablets, the estradiol is processed by the liver before entering the bloodstream. Progesterone increases the amount of oestrogen broken down in the liver (and thus less oestrogen actually enters the bloodstream).

- There are oestrogen receptors in the breast in which oestrogen is processed in order to grow the breast tissue. As the breast grows, it increases the number of oestrogen receptors. Progesterone actually reduces the number of oestrogen receptors in the breast tissue.

- Progesterone is converted into testosterone, thus increasing the amount of testosterone in the person's system.

Progesterone can also significantly impact mental health, in both cis and trans people.

Surgery

"Surgery is the time when having support is crucial, because your partner will be incapacitated, and they won't be reciprocally supporting you (as hopefully they would be usually). We were very grateful for support and advice from our community, particularly talking to people who had been through it already. I didn't know what was required of me and panicked a bit – ask lots of questions on forums if you can!" (Ricky)

The elation of the surgical referral in the trans person can, at the same time, create distress for the partner. Remember that it's completely normal. Surgery of any kind can be very scary and traumatic for anyone, and trans-related surgeries even more so.

"I hated all the surgeries, but did try very hard to support my partner and was there for him throughout. It was a huge mixture of feelings, especially in the early days, as each time he did something which helped him to become more 'him', it was a marvellous, joyful thing to see him so happy and calm. Although I was lucky to have some family and friends who were aware of what was happening, I found it incredibly hard not being allowed to discuss the surgeries with the people around me, and I remember having to hide from the neighbours after each one. Also, even though people knew about it, I didn't feel as though they understood or felt comfortable discussing it. I remember really resenting the fact that, for people whose partners have cancer, there is so much support and sympathy. It was horrible, as it was very important to me to feel that I had people around me I could belong to. I got incredibly stressed and pressured by the assumption that I would provide nursing care, as I felt revolted by the procedures that he was having. It had a huge emotional impact.

Now that we are separated, we are close friends, and I still talk with him and offer emotional support when he has revision surgeries. I feel okay with that, as I do still love him. However, I'm very glad I don't have to look at the results of the surgery any more." (Sasha)

It's normal that no matter how supportive you are and no matter how far you've come, surgery still feels a terrifying prospect.

"I just want to say that it's important to note that surgery alone is not the [be-all and end-all]...it takes time for a trans person's dysphoria to catch up with his or her body. Some of these processes take a lot of time, and it's a huge emotional and physical toll. Even after a person presents more how they want, it might catch them by surprise to see the person looking back at them from the mirror and for them to truly *see* and feel it. There is no overnight solution, so much patience is required, and lots of wonder and awe mark tiny progressions." (Julia)

While that is completely true in a terrifying way, the other part is that this doesn't change anything. Not really. You have been through so much more than this already; a physical change, no matter how terrifying, doesn't change who you both are as people.

"To be honest, by the time surgery was on the horizon, I'd had a long time to adjust (this happened about two years after transition was over). I was mostly looking forward to the correction of one last source of misery for her and sometimes both of us, and my reactions were more or less what would be expected from someone whose spouse was undergoing any type of major surgery: I was worried about anaesthesia, complications, infection and whether she'd be happy with the results. My one piece of advice in terms of practical recovery plans would be to stockpile as much of the necessary supplies as possible (our spare closet looked like a medical supply store!), because it may not be easy to find or buy more items once you're both embroiled in the nitty-gritty of recovery details. Oh, and neither of us were expecting the lifting restriction – no lifting over 10 pounds – when all our cats were 15 pounds or more, so I spent more time moving cats around than I'd imagined. Overall, the recovery was uneventful, and she was literally and figuratively back on her feet fairly quickly; she went back to work at four weeks post-op and did fine, although she still tired easily." (Tasha Martin)

Following the surgical referral, there is often a long wait for the surgical consultation and then a further wait between the consultation and the actual surgery date. One way to get through this interminable waiting is to keep busy.

> "When I found out that my partner's surgery was due to be scheduled in the next eight months, I felt a massive amount of anxiety – not sure why – and I still do. Part of it links to the change in sex and being 'presented' with a vagina rather than a penis. [I] think I'm also nervous about the process of transitioning being 'over' and what the next steps will be for us as a couple (e.g. not supporting her, etc.)." (Stevie)

Use the time as an opportunity to plan for every eventuality. Make sure that you both have current wills and have living wills set up. I know that it's morbid and awful to think about, but having that enormous step done can actually help you to get on with accepting that your partner's surgery isn't the worst thing that can happen. Once you have your affairs in order, you can start planning for the surgery and the aftercare.

The surgical consultation

The appointment with the surgeon can be very awkward and strange for the partner. The surgical consultation is usually a short appointment where the surgeon does an inspection of the trans person's body behind the curtain to determine the best type of surgery and surgical technique. A partner is not usually allowed behind the curtain during this examination.

Some anecdotal evidence suggests that surgeons can be very dismissive of trans people and even more dismissive of their partners. Some surgeons will not allow anyone but the trans person in the room for the consultation. Some surgeons will allow the partner in the room but will not speak to or make eye contact with the partner or will answer questions very abruptly.

"We went in to see the surgeon together; he put his arm around my partner, shook her hand, sat her down, sat down himself and totally ignored me. I sat myself down. The surgeon sat on a window seat grinning. At no time did he explain what operation he was doing. He made the statement that not everyone liked the finished results, but that wasn't his fault. [H]e said he had to tell us about what could go wrong [and] he mentioned a few medical terms; [he] said the percentages were low, but mentioned another side effect, and when it was obvious he was going to glance over it, I asked how we could tell if my partner had the side effect. [H]e looked at me with disgust and said, 'Poo will come out of her vagina.' Davina sat in total silence.

We were then told to go into the other room. The surgeon came with us, stopped grinning, [and] told my partner to drop her knickers and tights and get on the couch. The surgeon walked in and said, 'You have enough penile skin [and] you do not need electrolysis', and he walked out. My partner got off the bed and we went back into the room. She was told she needed a second referral, and as we were about to be dismissed, I asked the question about cosmetic surgery and said the surgical nurse had asked me to ask. [T]he surgeon stated, 'She would not be able to have penetrative sex.' My partner did not ask any questions. I was gobsmacked she had not asked any questions, but I did not know that she had been told she could not ask him any questions; she had to ask the clinicians." (Linda)

There are, however, surgeons who are supportive and accepting and will allow the partner to ask questions about the surgery and aftercare, after establishing the trans person's consent.

It is still worth going along with your partner to the surgical consultation. When it comes to the surgery, it's important for a trans person to have someone with them who can listen to what the surgeon says and recall it later on. This is especially true when some trans people find that the nervousness and excitement of finally seeing the surgeon can overwhelm them, and they sometimes can't recall all the details of what the surgeon said.

> "I left feeling numb, isolated and shocked, and [I] started to cry...every question I asked my partner, she did not know the answer. She was hurt by the way she had been treated by the surgeon; not once was she asked what she wanted, not once had she been asked about her lifestyle, not once had she been given a choice of operation. [S]he could not understand why she had been made to sit with two total strangers, [and] she had not comprehended anything that had been told to her in the meeting. She could not understand why I was so upset (I did protest in the reception) when they would not let me go with her. She was shell-shocked from the way she had been treated and kept saying it was similar to how she had been treated at the previous GIC...we thought we were having a private consultation with a surgeon, not going onto a conveyor system, [being] split up, [and] given photocopies of what to take into the hospital, what to buy and what to expect when you were in hospital." (Linda)

Some trans people prefer their partner not to accompany them to the surgical consultation, because they feel that it's too private; this is also completely understandable. Always make sure that you talk to your partner and let them know that you'd like to be there to support them and ensure you can have two sets of ears listening to the surgeon, but respect their wishes if they would prefer you not to attend.

Stopping hormones

For people who are taking estradiol, clinicians will require them to stop four to six weeks before the surgery to prevent the risk of deep vein thrombosis and blood clots. It's generally recommended to keep taking testosterone blockers during this time to prevent facial hair regrowth and other effects of testosterone. This can be an extremely stressful time for the relationship, because stopping estradiol and being on testosterone blockers can bring on menopause-like effects, such as hot flushes, irritability and fatigue.

There is not generally a requirement to stop taking testosterone before surgery; however, some surgeons will recommend it, as testosterone can increase bleeding.

Prepare for the hospital

The surgical team will provide you with a list of items required for the hospital stay; the following may also be worth considering:

- paperwork:
  - admission letter
  - name and address of GP
  - any current medication
  - consent form from the pre-admission clinic
- a bag or small suitcase with the essentials:
  - glasses/contact lenses
  - phone charger
  - cash for the hospital shop – be sure to have change, just in case there is a vending machine instead of a shop

- toiletries – toothbrush, toothpaste, soap, shampoo, etc.

- razor/s

- face cloth

- hairbrush

- clothes:

  - pyjamas – the hospital provides a gown, but many people feel much more comfortable once in their own clothes. Also, try to allow the nursing staff easy access to the surgical site. So, for example, for chest surgeries, consider pyjamas that open at the front, and for genital surgeries, try to avoid pyjama pants or shorts

  - gown and slippers to wear when walking around

  - underwear – for genital surgery, it is worth getting loose-fitting cotton underwear

  - loose clothing to wear on the way home

- entertainment – the hospital stay can be really boring, especially if it is for an extended number of days, so it's useful to have things to keep busy:

  - notepad and pen

  - book/s

  - tablet, laptop and respective chargers.

Travelling

The surgeons are based in specific hospitals across the country, and it will probably be necessary for your partner to travel to the specialist hospital for the surgery. You will be tempted to be there for the duration of their hospital stay, but you will not be able to do so. Try to arrange to be there for the check-in day (because there is usually a long wait between booking in to the hospital and actually going in for surgery), and then keep busy for the time that your partner is in surgery. Try to avoid waiting in the hospital. If it's at all possible, meet up with a friend who can just keep you busy. The wait can feel interminable, no matter how short the surgery. Once your partner is out of surgery, you may be able to see them (some hospitals will give you a call to let you know that they are out of surgery and recovering, but you may or may not be limited by visiting hours). Speak to the nursing staff to find out how it usually works so that you are prepared either way.

You will also need to take travelling arrangements into account; it's generally not advisable for people to take public transport after the more significant surgeries (especially genital surgeries, which will make sitting on a train or coach uncomfortable), so if at all possible, make arrangements for your partner to get home by car.

The surgical referral

The WPATH Standards of Care (World Professional Association for Transgender Health, 2011) advise that the clinician should determine eligibility for the specific surgery that a trans person chooses (more details on that in the following section) and make sure that the person is fully informed and ready for the surgery. Although the readiness of the person can vary, generally speaking, they need to have realistic expectations of what the surgery will do and how this will impact them. They will also need to have an aftercare plan in place and have considered their reproductive options.

The reality is usually that by the time a person has seen the gender clinician sufficiently to discuss surgery, they have thought out most of these considerations. Given that the waiting list for a surgical referral from the gender clinician can be up to 18 months (this is anecdotal, as no specific statistics are available), these decisions have often been well thought through by the time the surgical referral arrives. It is worth talking to your partner about it to make sure that you are both of a common understanding.

Criteria for getting surgical referrals

The WPATH Standards of Care (World Professional Association for Transgender Health, 2011) describe the criteria for getting a surgical referral in detail based on the type of surgery; however, for all the surgeries, the following criteria apply:

- persistent, well-documented gender dysphoria

- capacity to make a fully informed decision and to consent for treatment

- age of majority in a given country (if the patient is younger, follow the Standards of Care for children and adolescents)

- if significant medical or mental health concerns are present, they must be reasonably well controlled.

The following criteria differ based on the type of surgery:

- For the removal of breast tissue and creation of a masculine chest, there is no specific prerequisite for hormone therapy.

- For breast augmentation it is recommended that a person be on feminising hormones for at least 12 months, so that the maximum natural breast growth has happened (which prevents revision surgery being required to reshape the breasts due to changes from hormones). However, this is not an official criterion.

- For a hysterectomy (removal of the womb), ovariectomy (removal of the ovaries) and orchiectomy (removal of the testes), two referrals are required, and it is also required that a person be on continuous hormone therapy for at least 12 months to allow for a period where the effects on the reproductive organs are reversible prior to irreversible surgery. This requirement may not apply in some cases if the person is unable or unwilling to take hormones. The guidance does not make provision for non-binary people; this will need to be discussed and agreed with the clinician.

- For a metoidioplasty (creation of a phallus from the clitoris), phalloplasty (construction of a phallus from grafted material) and vaginoplasty (creation of the vagina, vulva and clitoris), two referrals are required, and the requirements are more strict. The criteria require a person to both have been on hormones and living in their gender role for at least 12 consecutive months. The guidance does not make provision for non-binary people; this will need to be discussed and agreed with the clinician.

Aftercare

The surgical team will also provide you with instructions for aftercare, but it's useful to think through the things that'll make the first week home as stress free as possible.

"I was terrified of what the scars would look like, and as somebody who has never cared for an adult previously, I was also terrified of what would be involved. The most helpful moment I had was when I took up a friend's offer of talking it through based on her experience of looking after her mother [after] a different type of surgery but involving a similar part of the body. It was this conversation which gave me the confidence I could do this...perhaps." (Sally Rush)

If you must take time off work, it is better for you to do so while your partner is home and recovering than while they are in hospital. For some of the surgeries, there is a requirement that people are not at home alone for the first week of recovery. If it's at all possible, staying home for the first two weeks is really useful, because the risk of complications is much lower after the first two weeks.

Once your partner has had surgery, it's vital to follow the surgeon's advice to make sure that they have a speedy recovery. It's also important to warn your GP about the surgery dates, etc., because if anything goes wrong, they will be your first port of call.

> "My wife went in for her vaginoplasty a few days before the surgeon went off to Thailand for the WPATH conference. While in hospital, she had uncontrolled bleeding; and instead of undressing the wound, they just kept wrapping her tighter and tighter in the bandages. When he did rounds the next day, all he said was 'You're not dead yet, so you'll be fine.' He then trotted off to Thailand and was not seen again.
>
> While in hospital, when they eventually removed the packing, it was clear that my wife was developing an infection, but the nursing staff kept ignoring her. When they did rounds to take her temperature, they'd do it about an hour after the paracetamol was given, so of course it never showed. They consistently misgendered her in hospital, and she never saw any doctors for the rest of her stay. She was discharged on the Saturday, still without having seen a doctor.
>
> We got an emergency appointment to see the GP the next day and he immediately prescribed her two sets of antibiotics (one for the bladder infection and one broad-spectrum antibiotic), which helped immensely.
>
> This was too late, however, as part of the skin graft failed and she faced years of trying to get back in for a revision surgery, where they said that they aren't really able to do anything and won't at all acknowledge what happened; it's not even in her notes.
>
> If it weren't for our GP, I think she would have died." (Jo)

Some practical things to think about are as follows:

- Food — make sure you have some meals that can be made relatively quickly and easily, to take the pressure off you. If you are the usual cook in the house, remember that you'll also be assisting your partner, so cooking might be more stressful than usual. If you aren't the usual cook, remember that the pressure of looking after your partner and needing to cook a meal can become overwhelming.

- Snacks — your partner may find that their appetite is different, either increased or decreased. Have some healthy snacks in the house for when they are feeling peckish.

- Cleanliness — it's important to make sure that the surgical areas remain as clean as possible. This may mean that you need an extra set of clean sheets and some easy cleaning products in the bathroom. Products to consider getting before your partner returns home are:

  - disposable bed pads/disposable baby changing mats (immensely useful and inexpensive)

  - disposable cleaning wipes for the bathroom.

Bear in mind that surgery is still traumatic for both of you. Make sure you keep communicating and are patient with each other. Once the first week is over, the healing accelerates, but your partner still must not overdo it, as this can have complications for the longer-term outcomes.

> "My partner is about to undergo a hysterectomy. It's taken a lot of preparation, due to him being my main carer." (Nicola Kalisky)

Take some time-outs, whether that is going out for a walk or reading a book in another room, without feeling guilty about it. You'll need time to recharge, too.

"I met him two months after top surgery and met in person two months after that, so he was finished healing. His chest is flat, and I like his results a lot, but he sometimes thinks a bit of tissue was missed and is occasionally dysphoric about his scars, because he wants to be able to take his shirt off without people staring. I actually quite like them, because it's part of him, and I don't think of what used to be there; to me, they're just scars. He wants to get them tattooed over – which I'd rather he didn't, but I'll support him with it, because I want him to be as comfortable as he can be within himself and it's his body anyway.

He's still recovering from stage one (UK) phalloplasty, and that has been challenging. He's had a few setbacks in his recovery, and his moods have been very up and down, because it's a stressful time, so the affection that would help keep me going isn't consistent, and we're both finding it hard. There are times when I feel that I can't do anything right; open communication is harder, because we're both quite sensitive right now, [and] his dysphoria is still pretty prominent, so any intimacy is [not on] the cards, etc. Whilst I wasn't expecting this to 'fix' everything, I was hoping it would ease it more for him than it has and that we could start working to get back to a place where we both seemed happier. I still have that hope, and I'm glad we're going through this, because I really do want him to feel content with himself, but having no clue about how long it could take to start noticeably improving isn't easy. He's a wonderful person [and] a great boyfriend, and I am in love with him, so any recovery challenges will be worth it to have him feel complete." (Shae)

13

Legal Transition

One of the biggest hurdles that must be faced is the mountain of paperwork that comes with changing a person's name and gender markers (where possible). In the UK, it is only possible to change gender markers for binary trans people, as there are no options outside of male and female for many institutions. Some banks do allow the title change to MX for non-binary people, but that's far from full legal recognition. While this is a chore, it can actually be an exciting time, because it marks that a person is officially telling the world at large about their true selves. For some trans people, changing names using online forms has made the process simpler, because they don't need to explain to a representative of a company who they are and come out as trans. For those changes that do need to be done over the phone, it can be enormously helpful for a partner to make those calls.

A note on language: to remain consistent with the language used by the government and institutions, I will use the term "acquired gender" to indicate the gender that the person is correcting. I recognise that this is at odds with the current thinking about trans identities, because the gender that was assigned at birth was incorrect and the changes serve to advise people of a trans person's correct gender. Where I use the term, I will indicate this in quotation marks.

As soon as you have a deed poll with your partner's new name on it, start collecting the utilities, bank statements and all other paperwork, as you will need to provide documentary evidence should they choose to apply for a GRC. I have listed the paperwork in the sequence that I suggest you follow.

Name change via deed poll

In order to change your name on your documents in the UK, you just need to complete a deed poll. If you are over the age of 18, there is no full legal process that needs to be followed, and it can be achieved inexpensively. It can be done on your own, but if you choose to use a solicitor or an online service, there may be a fee associated with that.

Making your own deed poll

If you make your own deed poll, you must use the following wording (HM Government, 2016b):

> "I [old name] of [your address] have given up my name [old name] and have adopted for all purposes the name [new name].
>
> Signed as a deed on [date] as [old name] and [new name] in the presence of [witness 1 name] of [witness 1 address], and [witness 2 name] of [witness 2 address].
>
> [your new signature], [your old signature]
>
> [witness 1 signature], [witness 2 signature]"

You will then need to get two people to witness your signature. Once you've done this, it should be accepted by most institutions.

Registering a deed poll

There is another way to complete a deed poll, and this will allow you to change your name on the public record; the process is more complex and will have an associated cost. It consists of three forms:

- Change of Name Deed, where you change your name

- Statutory Declaration, where you state that you hereby give up your previous name

- notice for the *London Gazette*, where you ask for your new name to be enrolled in the Senior Courts of England and Wales.

Once you've completed the three forms, they will need to be signed by witnesses. Your forms should be witnessed by someone who:

- is not a relative, your spouse or civil partner

- is a British or Commonwealth citizen

- has known you for more than ten years

- is a homeowner.

If you have not known anyone for ten years or more, an additional affidavit must be included which explains the reasons why. This will then be referred to the Senior Master for permission to enroll the change of name.

The Statutory Declaration must also be sworn to or affirmed in person with a solicitor, a Commissioner for Oaths or an Officer of the Senior Courts. The whole package is then posted to the HM Courts and Tribunals Service with the associated fee. Once it's been processed, you will receive the sealed deed poll, which you can then use as documentary evidence.

Utilities

Once you have a deed poll, one of the first places to change the name would be the utility bill and council tax. Many banks will request the deed poll and a proof of address with the new name on it as a proof of identity, so it's important to change the name on your utilities before going to the bank. Changing the name on the bill can often be done online, but if not, you can always call them to make the change. There should not be any costs involved for changing your name, but if company policy requires setting it up as a new account, you may need to pay any outstanding balances before making the change.

Voter's roll

Changing your name on the voter's roll can be done by going online[1] and completing a form (you may need your National Insurance Number and passport if you have them) or by contacting your local authority.

Bank

Changing a name at the bank should be as simple as providing the signed deed poll and a copy of a utility bill showing a proof of address. This does usually involve going into the bank to make the change.

Passport

To change your name and gender marker on a passport, you will need to complete the passport application form and submit the following:

- deed poll (showing the name change)

- utility bill (showing that the person is using their new name)

- proof of "acquired gender" (*one* of the following):

  - a letter from your doctor or medical consultant confirming your change of gender marker (and that the change is permanent)

---

1   www.gov.uk/register-to-vote

- a new birth certificate showing the "acquired gender"

- a GRC.

"I found out how she could change her name and went with her. When she told the private clinician, he gave her a letter to enable her to change her passport." (Linda)

If this is a first-time application for a passport, you will need to provide the above information in addition to the standard documentary evidence required when applying for a passport.

Driving licence

Changing your name and gender on your driving licence will involve filling in the required forms (which are available from the DVLA). To change your name, you will require a signed deed poll; however, to change your gender marker, a GRC is required. This means that you may need to change your driver's licence twice, once for a change of name and again once you have a GRC.

If you are changing your name on your driver's licence, you will also need to change the name on your vehicle's log book, which will involve posting the old log book with the change of name section completed (do not select the 'new keeper' box) and a note saying that you have changed your name.

Changing name with HMRC

You will also need to advise HM Revenue and Customs (HMRC) of your name change. This can be done online; however, HMRC will require you to provide them with proof of your name change (such as a deed poll and a utility bill reflecting the new name). Once you've done this, your name will be changed for income tax, national insurance, tax credits and benefits and services such as pensions. To change your gender marker with HMRC, you need to have a GRC.

Gender Recognition Certificate (GRC)

A GRC process is a legal requirement for someone to change their gender. This is governed by HM Courts and Tribunals. The Gender Recognition Panel is made up of legal and medical members who meet an average of three times a month and review approximately 14 applications per session (Gender Identity Research and Education Society, 2007). The applications are reviewed by civil servants who will make sure that all the information is in order before going to the Gender Recognition Panel.

Prior to December 2014, the Gender Recognition Act required that a marriage/civil partnership be dissolved before a GRC was granted, but provision has since been made for a spouse to provide a statutory declaration that they consent to the marriage's continuation. This change, although better than forcing the marriage or civil partnership to be dissolved, is still not fair to trans people; if the spouse does not provide consent, they will only be issued an interim certificate (with a specified time limit to either provide spousal consent or dissolve the marriage/civil partnership), thus holding the trans person hostage. This is known as the spousal veto.

> "I think there has also been a huge desire to hold on to my own sexual orientation, particularly as the law has not allowed me to (as I have had to move from civil partnership to marriage in order for my husband to be in a position where he can apply for his GRC)." (Sally Rush)

In order to apply for a GRC, the person will need to be over the age of 18, have lived in the "acquired gender" for at least two years and have an official diagnosis of gender dysphoria (HM Government, 2016a). This is so that the state can be comfortable that the change of gender marker is permanent. You will receive your documents back once the application has been reviewed by the Gender Recognition Panel. *All* the following original documents will need to be provided as part of the application:

- original (or certified copy) of your birth certificate

- copies of any official documents showing your name change (for example, your deed poll)

- proof that you've lived in your "acquired gender" for the required amount of time:

  - passport

  - driving licence

  - pay slips or benefit documents

  - utility bills, bank statements, etc. reflecting the new name for the whole time period

- medical reports (the format and details of these are included in the application packet)

  - a report from a gender specialist advising what medical treatments you have undergone

  - a report from your GP.

If you are married (in the UK), you will also need to provide:

- an original marriage/civil partnership certificate

- statutory declaration from a spouse that they wish the marriage to continue after the GRC is issued.

This collection of information must be sent to the Gender Recognition Panel, where they will review the documents you have provided and let you know if there is anything else that they need. They should also provide you with the date that your application will be decided. If you are successful, you will then receive the GRC (usually within two weeks) and information on how to apply for a new birth certificate and marriage/civil partnership certificate. Once the GRC has been approved, HMRC and other government bodies will be notified on your behalf, although the details of this are included in the information received back. It is rare, but if your application is declined, you will be provided with a reason and advised on how to appeal the decision.

Gender Recognition Act

It's important to know that once a person has a GRC, they are officially classed as the gender on the certificate, and the government and all other institutions should act as if they had been that gender since birth. There are however a number of provisions that the law (HM Government, 2004) makes which are counter to this aim, such as the following:

- Marriage and civil partnership: if you would like to get married, it will be in line with the current law (for example, only same-sex couples may get a civil union).

- Parenthood: the person will still be listed as their child's father or mother (this means, for example, that if a trans man gives birth to a child, they will still appear as the child's mother on the birth certificate).

- Social security benefits and pensions: for example, the pensionable age will be based on a person's "acquired gender".

- Inheritance and trusteeship: the law around inheritance once a person has changed gender is complex, so it's worth making sure you have legal assistance if this applies.

- Sports: sporting bodies may discriminate against trans participants even if they have a GRC.

- Gender-specific offences: the wording of this law is vague in that it says that if an offence is committed which can only be committed by someone who is of a specific gender (for example, a male) a person who has committed that offence will still be prosecuted even if they are in possession of a GRC.

While some of these provisions offer hardly any actual protection for trans people in all situations, the Act does state that it is against the law for anyone to out a trans person who has a GRC (HM Government, 2004), unless:

- the information does not enable the trans person to be identified (for example, statistics on the number of trans people in specific areas of the country)

- the trans person has given consent for the disclosure

- the person outing someone knew that the person was trans but didn't know they have a GRC (to be honest, this one baffles me)

- it's for the purposes of a court or tribunal

- it's for the purposes of investigating a crime

- the disclosure is made to the Registrar General

- it's for the purposes of social security or pensions

- the Secretary of State said that it could be done (for whatever reason).

Glossary

AFAB A person who was assigned female at birth; also referred to as FAAB (female assigned at birth), DFAB (designated female at birth) and CAFAB (coercively assigned female at birth).

Ally Someone who is supportive of trans people and trans people's rights; typically, cis or not affected by trans issues.

AMAB A person who was assigned male at birth; also referred to as MAAB (male assigned at birth), DMAB (designated male at birth) or CAMAB (coercively assigned male at birth).

Asexual Someone who does not experience sexual attraction.

Assigned at birth The gender that was given to a person when they were born.

Binary A system where there are only two options; used in the trans community to refer to the binary gender system, where people are either male or female (also known as the gender binary).

Cisgender Also abbreviated to cis; refers to someone whose gender identity matches the gender that was assigned at birth.

Cross-dresser A person who dresses in clothing stereotypically worn by the opposite sex, which is a form of gender expression.

Deadname To use a trans person's former name.

Drag queen/king Someone who cross-dresses as a form of performance.

Dysphoria A profound sense of unease.

Estradiol A form of oestrogen, the female sex hormone.

Gender The state of being male or female; generally refers to social and cultural differences (as opposed to sex, which refers to biological differences).

Gender dysphoria The profound sense of unease related specifically to a person's gender that was assigned at birth not matching their gender identity.

Gender expression How a person expresses their gender identity to others (such as name, pronouns, clothing, voice or body characteristics).

Gender identity An individual's internal sense of gender; gender identity is not always necessarily visible to others.

Gender Identity Clinic (GIC) A specialist clinic which provides services to trans people.

Gender nonconforming Refers to an individual whose gender expression is different from societal expectations related to gender.

Genderqueer Refers to individuals who identify anywhere on the gender spectrum (but not necessarily as either male or female).

Gender Recognition Certificate (GRC) A Gender Recognition Certificate is the certificate that trans people can apply for in the UK to change their gender marker for official purposes.

Heteromantic Someone who is romantically attracted to a person of the opposite gender (although may not be sexually attracted to them).

Heterosexual Someone who is sexually attracted to a person of the opposite gender.

Homoromantic Someone who is romantically attracted to a person of the same gender (although may not be sexually attracted to them).

Homosexual Someone who is sexually attracted to a person of the same gender.

Intersex Refers to people who are born with a variation in sex characteristics (i.e. external genitalia, chromosomes or internal reproductive systems that are not traditionally associated with the typical male or female configurations).

Misgender To use the wrong pronouns for a person, usually the pronouns that match the gender that was assigned at birth instead of the pronouns that match their gender identity. Referring to the person in the wrong gender can be highly traumatic (it is always best to ask).

MTF, M2F Male-to-female, a person who was given the gender of male when she was born but identifies as a female.

Non-binary An umbrella term for people who don't identify as entirely male or entirely female.

Panromantic Someone who is romantically attracted to a person irrespective of their gender (although may not be sexually attracted to them).

Pansexual Someone who is sexually attracted to a person irrespective of their gender.

Sexual orientation Sexual orientation refers to the orientation of the person in relation to who they are sexually attracted to. Homosexual refers to people who are attracted to people who are of the same gender, heterosexual refers to people who are attracted to people of the opposite gender, bisexual refers to people who are attracted to people of their own and other genders and pansexual refers to people who are attracted to people irrespective of gender. Transgender people may be straight, lesbian, gay, pansexual or bisexual.

Top surgery The removal of breast tissue and creation of a masculine chest.

Trans Used as shorthand to mean transgender or transsexual. Remember, trans is an adjective, so it is a trans woman (not transwoman) in the same way that it would be a short woman (not a shortwoman).

Trans man A person who was assigned female at birth but identifies as a man. Terms sometimes used: transgender man, FTM (an abbreviation for female-to-male) or simply man.

Trans woman A person who was assigned male at birth but identifies as a woman. Terms sometimes used: transgender woman, MTF (an abbreviation for male-to-female) or simply woman.

Transgender An umbrella term for people whose gender identity, expression or behaviour is different from their assigned sex at birth, including but not limited to cross-dressers, androgynous people, genderqueer people, non-binary people, transsexuals and gender nonconforming people. Some intersex people also identify as transgender.

Transition Transition includes some or all of the following steps: telling family, friends and co-workers; choosing and using a new name and new pronouns; dressing differently; changing name and/or sex on legal documents; hormone therapy; and surgery of some type.

Transphobia Discrimination or hatred toward a person because they are or are perceived to be trans.

Transsexual A term used for people whose gender identity is different from their assigned sex at birth. Often, transsexual people alter or wish to alter their bodies through hormones and/or surgery to match their bodies to their gender identity.

Transvestite An outdated term for a cross-dresser that is considered derogatory.

WPATH World Professional Association for Transgender Health, the leading organisation that deals with trans healthcare.

References

Benjamin, H. (1966). *The Transsexual Phenomenon*. New York: The Julian Press, Inc.

Curtis, R.J. (2009). *The Lowdown on Progesterone*. London: The London Gender Clinic. Accessed on 30/03/17 at https://uktrans.info/attachments/article/196/Progesterone.pdf

Ford, K.-K. (2000). "First, Do No Harm" – The Fiction of Legal Parental Consent to Genital-Normalizing Surgery on Intersexed Infants. *Yale Law & Policy Review, 19*(2), Article 7. Accessed on 30/03/17 at http://digitalcommons.law.yale.edu/ylpr/vol19/iss2/7

Gender Identity Research and Education Society (2007). Gender Recognition Panel. Accessed on 31/03/17 at www.gires.org.uk/law-archive/gender-recognition-panel

General Medical Council UK (2016). Trans Healthcare Treatment Pathways. Accessed on 30/03/17 at www.gmc-uk.org/guidance/ethical_guidance/28852.asp

HM Government (2004). *Gender Recognition Act 2004*. London: HMSO.

HM Government (2010, October). *Equality Act 2010*. London: HMSO.

HM Government (2016a). Apply for a Gender Recognition Certificate. Accessed on 04/04/17 at www.gov.uk/apply-gender-recognition-certificate/what-happens-next

HM Government (2016b). Change Your Name by Deed Poll. Accessed on 04/04/17 at www.gov.uk/change-name-deed-poll/overview

NHS North of Tyne Area Prescribing Committee (2016a). Guidelines for the Use of Feminising Hormone Therapy in Gender Dysphoria. Accessed on 04/04/17 at www.northoftyneapc.nhs.uk/wp-content/uploads/sites/6/2017/04/Gender-Dysphoria-Feminising-Hormones-Mar-2017.pdf

NHS North of Tyne Area Prescribing Committee (2016b). Guidelines for the Use of Masculinising Hormone Therapy in Gender Dysphoria. Accessed on 04/04/17 at www.northoftyneapc.nhs.uk/wp-content/uploads/sites/6/2017/04/Gender-Dysphoria-Masculinising-Hormones-Mar-2017.pdf

Oliven, J.F. (1965). *Sexual Hygiene and Pathology: A Manual for the Physician and the Professions.* Philadelphia: Lippincott.

Stonewall (2016). Stonewall Welcomes Clinical Condemnation of Trans "Cures". Accessed on 04/04/17 at www.stonewall.org.uk/media-centre/media-release/stonewall-welcomes-clinical-condemnation-trans-cures

Tanis, J., Grant, J.M., Mottet, L.A., Harrison, J., Herman, J. and Keisling, M. (2011). *Injustice at Every Turn: A Report of the National Transgender Discrimination Survey.* Washington: National Center for Transgender Equality.

UK Trans Info (2016). Current Waiting Times & Patient Population for Gender Identity Clinics in the UK. Accessed on 04/04/17 at https://uktrans.info/attachments/article/341/patientpopulation-oct15.pdf

World Health Organization (2016). *Genetic Components of Sex and Gender.* Geneva, Switzerland: World Health Organization. Accessed on 04/04/17 at www.who.int/genomics/gender/en/index1.html

World Professional Association for Transgender Health (2011). Standards of Care for the Health of Transsexual, Transgender, and Gender Nonconforming People. Accessed on 17/04/17 at https://s3.amazonaws.com/amo_hub_content/Association140/files/Standards%20of%20Care%20V7%20-%202011%20WPATH%20(2)(1).pdf

Resources

Support spaces

Distinction Partner Support

Distinction is the only active group for people whose partners are transitioning. It is run as a secret Facebook group (so that the group's membership is not visible to anyone outside of the group) and currently has in excess of 100 active members. The group provides peer support, answers to questions and a sense of community.

www.distinctionsupport.org

TranzWiki

TranzWiki is a directory of trans-related groups in the UK. It contains the details of organisations involved in support and campaigning for trans people in the UK and was developed by the Gender Identity Research and Education Society.

www.gires.org.uk/the-wiki

Partners' websites and blogs

It's All About My Lucy (UK)

A blog by a woman who's the partner of a trans woman. She writes about her experiences as the transition progresses and other parts of family life.

http://itsallaboutmylucy.blogspot.co.uk

First Time Second Time (US)

A blog by a queer mother and a trans father who have two children. The blog started in 2008 and the couple have documented both their life trying to conceive pre-transition as well as their parenting post-transition.

https://firsttimesecondtime.com

Maven of Mayhem (US)

A blog by Amanda Jetté Knox, who is a writer, human rights advocate, parent to a trans child and a wife to a trans woman. She documents their life, the challenges they face and the celebration of their family.

www.amandajetteknox.com

Helen Boyd (US)

Helen Boyd wrote two of the first books by the partner of a trans woman, *My Husband Betty* (2004) and *She's Not the Man I Married: My Life with a Transgender Husband* (2007). She writes opinion pieces on current issues in the trans community.

www.myhusbandbetty.com

Books

Trans Bodies, Trans Selves: A Resource for the Transgender Community

Laura Erickson-Schroth (Editor), OUP USA, 10 July 2014, ISBN 0199325359

An essential owner's manual for trans people's bodies. Covers all aspects of trans bodies, from self-identification, intersectionality, health and wellness, relationships and life stages.

Trans-Kin: A Guide for Family and Friends of Transgender People: Volume 1

Dr Eleanor A. Hubbard (Author), Cameron T. Whitley (Author), Bolder Press, 9 Aug. 2012, ISBN 0615630677

A collection of stories by significant others, friends, families and allies of trans people.

Love, Always: Partners of Trans People on Intimacy, Challenge and Resilience

Jordon Johnson (Author, Editor), Becky Garrison (Editor), Transgress Press, 12 Mar. 2015, ISBN 0986084409

A collection of stories written by partners of trans people presenting the impact of the transition on their family and relationships.

A Love Less Ordinary: Sharing Life, Laughter and Handbags with My Transgender Partner

Laura Newman (Author), Bramley Press, 20 Nov. 2012, ISBN 0957132522

A memoire of the partner of a trans person and how the transition helped her discover how to live authentically.

Transgender 101: A Simple Guide to a Complex Issue

Nicholas Teich (Author), Columbia University Press, 13 Apr. 2012, ISBN 0231157134

A simple and easy-to-understand perspective on transgenderism and its psychological, social and physical processes.

UK trans organisations

a:gender

Phone: 0114 207 2547
Email: agender@homeoffice.gsi.gov.uk
Website: www.agender.org.uk

AffirmNI

AffirmNI
5 Glenabbey Garden
Londonderry
BT48 8GW

Phone: 07542 666345
Email: info@affirmni.co.uk
Website: www.affirmni.co.uk

Chrysalis Transsexual Support Groups

Community Wellbeing Centres
10 Richmond Terrace
Blackburn
BB1 7BD

Phone: 01254 675183
Email: chrysalis@transsexualinfo.co.uk
Website: www.transsexualinfo.co.uk

cliniQ

56 Dean Street
London
WC1D 6AQ

Phone: 07545 143797
Email: admin@cliniq.org.uk
Website: www.cliniq.org.uk

ELOP

ELOP Centre
56–60 Grove Road
London
E17 9BN

Phone: 020 8509 3898
Email: info@elop.org
Website: www.elop.org

Equality Network

Equality Network
30 Bernard Street
Edinburgh
EH6 6PR

Phone: 0131 467 6039
Email: en@equality-network.org
Website: www.equality-network.org

GenderAgenda

Registered Office
4 Crown Point Drive
Norwich
NR14 8RR

Phone: 07808 970429
Email: info@genderagenda.net
Website: www.genderagenda.net

Gender Essence Support Services

9–13 Waring Street
Belfast
BT1 2DX

Phone: 07487 683912
Email: info@genderessence.org.uk
Website: www.genderessence.org.uk

The Gender Identity Research and Education Society

Melverley
The Warren
Ashtead
Surrey
KT21 2SP

Website: www.gires.org.uk

GenderJam NI

Belfast Trans Resource Centre
98 University Street
Belfast
BT7 1HE

Phone: 028 90 996 819
Email: info@genderjam.org.uk
Website: www.genderjam.org.uk

The Kite Trust

Office A
Dales Brewery
Cambridge
CB1 2LJ

Phone: 01223 369508
Email: office@syacambs.org
Website: www.thekitetrust.org.uk

National LGB&T Partnership

Phone: 020 7064 6506
Email: nationallgbtpartnership@gmail.com
Website: https://nationallgbtpartnership.org

Navigate

Space for Change
14 Windlesham Avenue
Brighton
BN1 3AH

Email: navigatebrighton@gmail.com
Website: https://navigatebrighton.wordpress.com

Pink Therapy

BCM 5159
London
WC1N 3XX

Phone: 020 7836 6647
Email: webadmin@pinktherapy.com
Website: www.pinktherapy.com

The Rainbow Project

c/o 42 Bradshaw Avenue
Treeton
S60 5QJ

Phone: 07443 932424
Email: therainbowproject@outlook.com
Website: www.therainbowproject.org.uk

safeT: Strength Awareness Freedom and Empowerment for Transgender People

Phone: 07910 633365
Email: info@safetuk.org
Website: www.safetuk.org

Stonewall

Tower Building
York Road
London
SE1 7NX

Phone: 020 7593 1850
Email: info@stonewall.org.uk
Website: www.stonewall.org.uk

Transcend

Derbyshire Friend
2–3 Friary Street
Derby
DE1 1JF

Phone: 01332 207704
Email: info@transcend.org.uk
Website: www.transcend.org.uk

Unity Group Wales

Unity LGBT Centre
High Street
Swansea
SA1 1LN

Phone: 01792 346299
Email: info@unitygroup.wales
Website: www.unitygroup.wales

Fostering and adoption support

New Family Social

UK organisations led by LGBT foster carers and adopters. They provide help and support on adoption and fostering.

New Family Social
Harvey's Barn
Park End
Swaffham Bulbeck
CB25 0NA

Phone: 0843 2899457
Email: membership@newfamilysocial.org.uk
Website: www.newfamilysocial.org.uk

About the Author

Jo is a partner of a trans woman and identifies as non-binary (they/them/their pronouns). They supported their partner through transition and have been involved in the trans community in various forms in both South Africa and the UK.

In 2014, dissatisfied with partner groups that only allowed cis people or catered to wives struggling with their partner's cross-dressing, they decided to start Distinction Trans Couple Support, a secret Facebook group for people (irrespective of gender) whose partners are trans. In the few years that it has been running, it has added over a hundred members who found the group through word of mouth. All the individual contributions have come from people who have voluntarily provided submissions, not from discussion within the group.

In the course of being involved in the trans community, they have spoken to many partners and discussed all the things that a partner may want to know or to talk about with other partners.

They are also the author of the book *Queer Paganism: A Spirituality That Embraces All Identities* (ISBN-10: 1533441448).

Index